The Complete Book of

CUT FLOWER CARE

The Complete Book of

CUT FLOWER CARE

MARY JANE VAUGHAN

TIMBER PRESS
Portland, Oregon

Copyright ©1988 by Mary Jane Vaughan
Illustrations by Helen Senior

First published in 1988 by Christopher Helm (Publishers) and
Timber Press

Paperback edition printed in 1998 by
Timber Press, Inc.
The Haseltine Building
133 S.W. Second Avenue, Suite 450
Portland, Oregon 97204, U.S.A.

ISBN 0-88192-412-1

Printed in Hong Kong

Library of Congress Cataloging-in-Publication Data

Vaughan, Mary Jane.
        The complete book of cut flower care / Mary Jane Vaughan. —
    Paperback ed.
            p.   cm.
        Includes bibliographical references (p.   ) and indexes.
        ISBN 0-88192-412-1 (pbk.)
        1. Cut flowers. 2. Cut foliage. 3. Cut flowers—Postharvest
    technology. 4. Cut Foliage—Postharvest technology. I. Title.
    SB449.V37   1998
    635.9'666—dc21   97-24638
                                                                CIP

CONTENTS

INTRODUCTION

In the last fifteen to twenty years, the flower industry has gone through dramatic changes. New scientific developments in horticulture, advances in refrigeration, and more frequent and relatively cheap air transport, have made it possible to buy a large variety of flowers all year round, from almost anywhere in the world. The customer has come to expect a large range of flowers throughout the year, regardless of season. The fact that the flowers may be flown in from the other side of the world no longer means that they are a luxury item, or even that they are more expensive than those grown locally.

As a result, the traditional concept, of the local small grower supplying his area with seasonal flowers, is being replaced by specialised horticultural farms which, in an ideal climate, can mass produce flowers at a quality and price with which the non-specialised nursery is not always able to compete. This means that only rarely are flowers sent directly from the nursery to the local market. The chain of distribution of cut flowers has grown to include shippers, agents, exporters, importers and wholesalers, one or all of whom may have handled the flowers before they reach the flower shop.

These stages of distribution are a chain, in which each and every step affects the final quality and longevity of the flowers. The best quality flowers may have left the nursery, but if, on the way, they have been kept too long or under inadequate conditions, they will arrive in a poor state. Likewise, no matter how well the wholesaler takes care of his flowers, if they have been cut too early, they will lack quality.

A thorough knowledge of how to handle and care for cut flowers, simply means better, longer-lasting flowers. For the customer, it means extra enjoyment; for the retail trade, it can mean extra profits.

GLOSSARY

Bract: a modified leaf beneath a flower. In many cases the flowers themselves are hidden or partially hidden, and the bracts are the main feature of the flower head (e.g. proteas).

Calyx: small, protective leaf or outer case around a flower.

Cluster: a group of flowers, tightly or loosely packed.

Corolla: the petals as a whole.

Double flowers: flowers with multiple rows of petals.

Floret: a small flower, usually grouped together with others, to form a larger flower mass.

Panicle: a branching raceme.

Raceme: flowers grouped alongside a stem, each on a short stalk.

Single flowers: flowers with a single row of petals.

Spadix: a fleshy spike of tiny flowers (e.g. anthuriums).

Spathe: a leaf-like part of a plant, surrounding the spadix (e.g. anthuriums).

Spike: flowers grouped alongside and growing directly from the stem (e.g. gladioli).

Style: the part of the flower which extends from the ovary and bears the stigma.

ACKNOWLEDGEMENTS

To Jimmy Vaughan. His encouragement
and support made this book possible.

Care of Cut Flowers in the Home

Flowers bought for home enjoyment will most likely have been 'worked on', or handled, by the florist, and should be in optimum condition. Nevertheless, a few general tips will help to ensure that the flowers open up and last to their full potential.

HOME CARE FOR ALL CUT FLOWERS

Cut the Stem Ends

Cut 1 in (2.5 cm) or so off the end of the stem, at an angle, using a sharp knife. This will ensure that the stem ends are open and will take up water.

Remove Lower Foliage

Carefully remove all the foliage that would otherwise be in the water, as it may rot, encouraging the proliferation of bacteria in the water. Remove any excess foliage as well, as a great deal of water is lost through the leaves.

Place the Flowers in Water with Flower Food

Place the flowers in a clean vase with warm water, and add flower food. All good florists will provide you with a sachet of flower food; or it can be homemade — mix equal amounts of water and lemon fizzy drink, and add a drop of bleach (see Appendix I). Flower food keeps the water in the vase clean and fresh, and provides the flower with nutrients, both of which promote flower opening and a longer vase life.

Where to Place the Flowers

Choose a light, cool spot to place your arrangement. Avoid direct sunlight, and proximity to heaters, air conditioning units and draughts, as these will dehydrate the flowers. Do not place your flowers next to ripening fruit and vegetables, as these give out a ripening hormone (called ethylene gas; see Appendix III) that will hasten deterioration of the flowers.

Remove Damaged Flowers and Foliage

Remove any flowers or leaves that are damaged or that wilt, as they may affect the life of the rest of the flowers.

Change the Water and Re-cut the Stems

Frequent changes of water and re-cutting the stem ends will ensure a good, steady flow of water up the stem. If you are not using cut flower food, change the water and re-cut the stems every 2 days. If you are, then every 5 days is enough.

If you have received an arrangement of flowers in flower foam, water the foam daily, as it dries out quickly.

Special home care, in addition to the above recommendations, is required for some cut flowers. The details are given under the relevant individual listings in the A-Z.

SPECIAL CARE FOR ORCHIDS

Orchids benefit from extra special care. The details are given here, rather than repeated under each individual orchid.

Contrary to general belief, orchids have a good vase life, as long as they are kept in water. When you buy orchids, the stems may come in a water tube, or wrapped in wet cotton wool. This should be removed, and the stems re-cut and placed in fresh water with flower food as soon as possible. Orchids should be kept away from heat, draughts, fans, air conditioning units and anything that may cause moisture loss. Frequent misting of the flowers with water is recommended. If they look limp, place them in water — flower head and all — for up to one hour.

Orchids should also be kept away from fruit, vegetables and decaying flowers, as orchids are especially susceptible to ethylene gas.

MYTHS AND FACTS

There are many popular formulas for flower care. But are they myths or facts? Most have a certain basis of truth to them; some are ineffective; and a few are actually harmful to the flowers.

Cut the Stems, Crush, Slit or Sear them with a Flame?

A clean cut, at an angle, will expose open strands of the stem to water, and prevent heavy stems from sealing to the bottom of the vase. Crushing or slitting the stems may close up these strands and obstruct the water flow. It has been proved, for example, that the vase life of roses can be reduced by half, when the stem ends are crushed instead of cut.

Some stems that 'bleed' when cut (i.e. lose latex) need to be seared with a flame or placed in boiling water for a few seconds, to seal in the latex. Once this has been done, do not re-cut again. If using boiling water, protect the flowers and leaves from the steam.

Cut Stems Underwater?

It is advisable — though not essential — to cut the stem ends when they are underwater. This will ensure that water, instead of air, travels up the stem, as air can settle at the base of the flower, and not allow water up to the flower head. This is especially the case in roses.

Bleach, Lemonade, 7-Up, Aspirins, Pennies, Flower Food, Sugar, Alcohol?

Adding pennies and aspirins to the water has no visible effect on the longevity of cut flowers. The idea is not without foundation (it helps prevent the growth of micro-organisms in the water) but the results are hardly noticeable. A drop of bleach, clean containers, or the antiseptic in the flower food, do a more thorough job.

Alcoholic drinks do, in fact, provide good nutrients for the flowers as they contain sugar. But the flower is just as happy with sugar or lemonade.

The More Water in the Vase, the More the Flowers will Drink?

A flower takes up water in the same way that a straw does. Only so much goes up the stem, and the amount of water in the vase will not increase the amount of water a flower will drink.

Some flowers, such as tulips, are 'heavy drinkers', so check the water level frequently to make sure that the stem ends are covered.

Warm, Cold or Boiling Water?

Warm water is advisable (it should feel comfortable when run on the back of your hand), as warm water has less air than cold water, and travels more easily up the stem. Ice cold or boiling water is not advisable, although boiling water can be used for a few minutes to soften the tissue of woody stems, to ease the water flow up the stem.

Metal, Plastic or China Containers?

Plastic or china containers are preferable as they are easily cleaned. Metal containers are difficult to clean, and the metal can sometimes neutralise the effect of the flower food.

Place the Flowers in a Refrigerator?

Home refrigerators do not provide humidity, and placing flowers in them can cause the flowers to dehydrate. If it is necessary to keep a corsage, bouquet or other small arrangement cool and fresh for a few hours, it can be placed in a refrigerator, provided the stems are in water, and the flowers are wrapped in a plastic bag to maintain moisture.

Water Softeners?

Although 'hard' water is harmful to flowers, the use of water softeners is not recommended as they contain salts that will damage the flowers.

Slitting or Piercing the Base of a Tulip?

This method of straightening a tulip has not been shown to have any effect. The best way to straighten up bent tulips (or most other bulbous flowers) is by wrapping them tightly in wet paper and placing in water with light directly above them. Since tulips curve towards light, they will become sturdy and straight by drinking water with light directly over them.

A-Z of
Cut Flowers

ACONITUM
Monk's hood

Adonis vernalis

FAMILY: Ranunculaceae
BOTANICAL NAME: *Aconitum napellus*, *Aconitum arendsii* and hybrids
DESCRIPTION: Spikes with dark blue to violet, hooded flowers, 1-1½in (2.5-4cm) across, on stems 3ft (1m) long, when cut.
   All parts of the plant are poisonous.
TIME TO BUY: When the lower florets have begun to open.
AVAILABILITY: Summer to autumn.
VASE LIFE: Approximately 10 days, during which time the flowers will continue to open.
TRADE CARE: Best kept at 45-50°F (7-10°C). Lower temperatures may cause frost damage, resulting in blackening of the petals. Storage is not recommended.
SUITABLE FOR DRYING

ADONIS

FAMILY: Ranunculaceae
BOTANICAL NAME: *Adonis amurensis*
DESCRIPTION: Single or double, daisy-like flowers, 2in (5cm) across, appear at the end of short (12in, 30cm) stems. The flowers are yellow.
TIME TO BUY: The petals should have opened but should not be lying flat.
AVAILABILITY: Early summer.
VASE LIFE: 5-6 days.
SPECIAL HOME CARE: Avoid draughts as these can dehydrate the flowers.
TRADE CARE: Best kept at 34-36°F (1-2°C) if possible (if not, 36-41°F (2-5°C) will do) and place in water as soon as possible. Storage is not recommended.

AGAPANTHUS
African lily, Lily of the Nile

FAMILY: Liliaceae
BOTANICAL NAME: *Agapanthus africanus*, *A. umbellatus*
DESCRIPTION: Small, long, funnel-shaped flowers appear in a round cluster 6-8in (15-20cm) wide at the end of a thick, single stem. When cut, the overall length is about 3ft (1m). The flowers are mainly blue or violet-blue such as 'Blue Triumphator', 'Blue Globe' and 'Intermedia'; white varieties, such as 'Alba' are less common. There are some dwarf varieties but these are not very popular as cut flowers.
TIME TO BUY: When one-third of the flowers on the cluster are open.
AVAILABILITY: Late spring and summer.
VASE LIFE: 4-6 days opening, and a further 7-14 flowering.
SPECIAL HOME CARE: Frequent re-cutting of stem ends and addition of flower food will help keep petal drop to a minimum, and promote opening of all the flowers on the cluster.
TRADE CARE: Best kept at 34-41°F (1-5°C). Place in water as soon as possible. The varieties 'Blue Globe' and 'Blue Triumphator' are less prone to petal drop. Handle carefully to avoid petal damage. Growers usually ship the flowers with a protective mesh around each flower head.

AGERATUM

FAMILY: Compositae
BOTANICAL NAME: *Ageratum conyzoides*, *A. houstonianum*
DESCRIPTION: Blue or white flower clusters, 2in (5cm) across, appear at the end of a short stem (usually no more than 8-12in (20-30cm) long).

TIME TO BUY: When the flowers are starting to open.
AVAILABILITY: Late summer and early autumn.
VASE LIFE: Approximately 10 days.
TRADE CARE: Best kept at 34-36°F (1-2°C). Storage is not recommended.

ALCHEMILLA
Lady's mantle

FAMILY: Rosaceae
BOTANICAL NAME: *Alchemilla mollis*
DESCRIPTION: Branched heads formed by tiny, yellowish-green star-shaped flowers. When cut, the overall length is 12-20 in (30-50 cm).
TIME TO BUY: When the flowers have just opened.
AVAILABILITY: Summer.
VASE LIFE: Approximately 1 week.
TRADE CARE: Best kept at 34-36°F (1-2°C). Storage is not recommended.
SUITABLE FOR DRYING

ALLIUM
Ornamental onion flower

FAMILY: Liliaceae
BOTANICAL NAME: *Allium* species
DESCRIPTION: Tight or loose, round clusters of small, star-shaped flowers that are usually purple, although some varieties are red, white or yellow. Both flower head and stem length varies according to the variety.
1. Varieties with tight round clusters forming an almost perfect circle include:
A. *giganteum*: Giant variety, tight, purple cluster up to 6 in (15 cm) in diameter. Stem length reaches up to 4¼ft (130 cm).
A. *sphaerocephalum*: Tight, blue-purplish cluster up to 2 in (5 cm) in diameter, average stem length 20 in (50 cm).
2. Varieties with loose clusters of star-shaped flowers include:
A. *moly*: Bright yellow flowers appear on a loose, terminal cluster up to 2 in (5 cm) across, on a short stem no more than 12 in (30 cm) in length.
A. *neapolitanum*: Similar to A. *moly*, with white flowers.
A. *oreophilum*: Similar to A. *moly*, with pink flowers.
Although related to garlic, allium flowers do not smell of garlic unless severely bruised.
TIME TO BUY: When one-third of the blooms on the cluster have opened.

AVAILABILITY: Late spring and summer.
VASE LIFE: Up to 2 weeks.
TRADE CARE: Best kept at 36-41°F (2-5°C). At these temperatures they can be held for 3 days dry or 4-6 days in water.
SUITABLE FOR DRYING (mainly *Allium sphaerocephalum*)

ALSTROEMERIA
Peruvian lily, Ulster Mary

FAMILY: Amaryllidaceae
BOTANICAL NAME: *Alstroemeria* species, mainly A. *aurantiaca*
DESCRIPTION: 3-7 irregular, trumpet-shaped flowers, 1½ in (4 cm) wide, borne at the end of short flower stalks that spray off a single stem. The flowers are bi-coloured or multi-coloured and are streaked, striped or marbled. The stems, when cut, are 1-3 ft (30-100 cm) long.
The main varieties are: 'Harmony' (bronze), 'Carmen' (orange), 'Jacqueline' (pink), 'King Cardinal' (red), 'Canaria' (yellow), 'Paloma' (cream) and 'Lilac Glory' (purple). The orchid types (such as 'Orchid' (yellow), 'Zebra' (yellow) and 'Canaria') are losing in popularity because their leaves do not keep as well as the butterfly types (such as 'Rosario' (yellow) and 'Jacqueline' (pink)), hybrids (such as 'Pink Triumph') and 'Carmen' types (such as 'Red Valley en Cana'). There are also many new Dutch hybrids.
TIME TO BUY: When the first bud has opened, and the majority are showing colour.
AVAILABILITY: All the year round.
VASE LIFE: Approximately 10 days, during which time the flowers will continue to open up.
SPECIAL HOME CARE: Remove any excess foliage.
TRADE CARE: Best kept at 36-41°F (2-5°C). At these temperatures they can be held for 2-3 days in water.
The leaves are more delicate than the flowers, so special care is needed when handling them, i.e. it is best not to stack them.
Alstromerias are prone to yellowing of the leaves. Premature yellowing usually indicates a fault at the nursery stage, but pre-treatment techniques are now proving effective.
These flowers are graded according to the stem length, as well as by the number of florets per stem.

AMARANTHUS
Cat's tail, Love-lies-bleeding

Amaranthus caudatus

For Globe amaranth, see Gomphrena
FAMILY: Amaranthaceae
BOTANICAL NAME: *Amaranthus caudatus* and hybrids
DESCRIPTION: Drooping red flower racemes, up to 16 in (40 cm) in length, on stems that, when cut, are up to 3 ft (1 m) long. Other varieties (less common) have erect and brush-like flower racemes, up to 6 in (15 cm) in length, that are red, creamy or green, and stand at the end of tall stems.
TIME TO BUY: When the flower stems have developed.
VASE LIFE: Approximately 1 week.
TRADE CARE: Best kept at 36-41°F (2-5°C). Storage is not recommended.
SUITABLE FOR DRYING

AMARYLLIS AND HIPPEASTRUM

FAMILY: Amaryllidaceae
BOTANICAL NAME: *Amaryllis belladonna* and *Hippeastrum* hybrid. The name *Amaryllis* causes some confusion: it is usually used as a common name both for *Amaryllis belladonna* (the true *Amaryllis*), and for *Hippeastrum*, a flower closely related to *Amaryllis*. The latter is more commonly used as a cut flower. To add to the confusion, *Amaryllis belladonna* is sometimes called the Belladonna Lily.

Hippeastrum, sometimes wrongly spelt Hyppeastrum, is commonly known simply as Amaryllis.
DESCRIPTION: *Amaryllis belladonna* has 6-12, trumpet-shaped flowers, each 4-5 in (10-12 cm) across, on a single thick, leafless stem, 14-20 in (30-50 cm) long. The flowers are pink, shades of red or white.

Hippeastrum also has a thick, hollow stem, with 4-6 larger, trumpet-shaped flowers, 5-6 in (12-15 cm) across. The flowers are white, pink or red, and the average stem length is 20-28 in (50-70 cm). *Hippeastrum gracilis* has thinner stems with smaller flowers. Hippeastrum hybrids are larger than *A. belladonna*.
TIME TO BUY: Amaryllis: when only one flower has opened; Hippeastrum: when at least two of the flowers are showing colour and stand loose.
AVAILABILITY: Amaryllis: Summer to autumn; hippeastrum: winter and early spring.
VASE LIFE: Up to 10 days during opening stage; a further week once open.
SPECIAL HOME CARE: Keep away from cold and handle with care.

It is often recommended that the hollow stem be filled with water, and 'plugged' with cotton wool — this is time-consuming and unnecessary if your flowers are healthy and sturdy. When the water in the vase is changed, amaryllis stems expel the water held in the hollow stem, and take in water again when placed in fresh water. In water, the base of the stem will turn red and curl up — this does not affect the keeping quality of this flower.
TRADE CARE: Amaryllis and hippeastrum should be kept at 41-50°F (5-10°C). Lower temperatures may result in discoloration of the petals and the buds may not open; higher temperatures, 55-59°F (13-15°C), should also be avoided. At these temperatures, amaryllis can be kept dry for 7-10 days. Once in water, they will begin to open.

Unlike most bulbous flowers, amaryllis does not open immediately. The addition of cut flower food — if possible bulb flower food — is recommended.

Amaryllis are graded according to the number of flowers on the stem.

Handle these flowers with care — they bruise easily.

AMMOBIUM
Winged everlasting

Ammobium alatum

FAMILY: Compositae
BOTANICAL NAME: *Ammobium alatum* 'Majus'
DESCRIPTION: Tiny, white, everlasting flowers with yellow centres on winged stems that are no more than 12-16 in (30-40 cm) in length.
TIME TO BUY: When most of the flowers are fully open.
AVAILABILITY: Summer and autumn.
VASE LIFE: Approximately 1 week.
TRADE CARE: Best kept at 36-41°F (2-5°C). Storage is not recommended.
SUITABLE FOR DRYING

ANANAS
Ornamental pineapple

FAMILY: Bromeliaceae
BOTANICAL NAME: *Ananas sogeinaria*
DESCRIPTION: Large, pink flower head, up to 10 in (25 cm) long, with a similar shape to the edible pineapple. It appears from the centre of a rosette of leaves. The total height is usually 16-24 in (40-60 cm). Both flower size and stem length can vary considerably.
TIME TO BUY: When fully developed.
VASE LIFE: 2-3 weeks. No special care is required.
TRADE CARE: Can be kept at room temperature. They can last for up to one week without water, if the temperature is kept cool.
SUITABLE FOR DRYING

ANAPHALIS
Pearl everlasting

Anaphalis margaritacea

FAMILY: Compositae
BOTANICAL NAME: *Anaphalis* species
DESCRIPTION: Flat racemes made of small white flowers, at the end of short stems 6-10 in (15-25 cm) in length.
TIME TO BUY: When the flowers have opened.
AVAILABILITY: Autumn.
VASE LIFE: 7-10 days.
TRADE CARE: Best kept at 36-41°F (2-5°C). Storage is not recommended.
SUITABLE FOR DRYING

ANEMONE
Windflower, Lily of the field, Poppy anemone

FAMILY: Ranunculaceae
BOTANICAL NAME: *Anemone coronaria*
DESCRIPTION: Cup-shaped flowers, 2½-3 in (6-8 cm) wide, that open up almost flat when mature. There are single, double and semi-double forms. They appear at the end of a thin stem, reaching an average height of 12 in (30 cm). ('Mona Lisa' varieties are taller — on average 20 in (50 cm) tall, with 4-5 in (10-12 cm) flowers). The petals, which surround a dark centre, come in shades of purple, blue, red, pink and white.

Developed from *A. coronaria*, there are now de Caen single forms, such as 'His Excellency' (red), 'The Bride' (white) and 'Blue Poppy' (blue) and St Brigid double forms, such as 'Lord Lieutenant' (blue) and 'Governor' (red), though mixtures are the most widely grown. The 'St Priam' and the seed-raised 'Mona Lisa' strains are now becoming much more popular.
TIME TO BUY: The petals should have started to separate from the centre, but not yet be lying flat.
AVAILABILITY: Mainly late winter through spring.
VASE LIFE: 5-6 days (and up to 10 days).
SPECIAL HOME CARE: Check the level of water frequently as anemones are 'heavy drinkers'. Keep away from draughts, direct sunlight and excess heat. They tend to curve towards light, so take care to place the flowers in an even lighted spot in order to avoid stem curvature. If they are very bent on arrival, the best way to straighten them is to place them, tightly wrapped in wet paper, facing inwards, in a cool dark spot in water. This way they will straighten up as they drink water.
TRADE CARE: Best kept at 36-41°F (2-5°C) (although a temperature closer to 41°F (5°C) is recommended). Place in water as soon as possible. Storage is not recommended. The flowers tend to close up when refrigerated, but will open up once placed at room temperature.
SUITABLE FOR DRYING

ANTHEMIS

Anthemis tinctoria

FAMILY: Compositae
BOTANICAL NAME: *Anthemis tinctoria*
DESCRIPTION: Terminal, daisy-like flowers, 2-2½ in (5-6 cm) across, on stems up to 16 in (40 cm) in height. The flowers are mainly yellow with yellow centres, less commonly white and cream with yellow centres.
TIME TO BUY: When the flowers are starting to open.
AVAILABILITY: Summer.
VASE LIFE: Approximately 10 days.
TRADE CARE: Best kept at 36-41°F (2-5°C). Storage is not recommended.
SUITABLE FOR DRYING

ANTHURIUM
Painter's palette, Flamingo flower

FAMILY: Araceae
BOTANICAL NAME: *Anthurium andreanum, A. scherzerianum*
DESCRIPTION: Anthurium flowers consist of a modified, shiny and colourful leaf, called a spathe, usually heart-shaped or arrow-shaped, with a cylindrical long spadix that is usually yellow. The size of the

flower can vary between 2¾-6in (7-15cm) or more, and the length of the stem, between 1-2ft (30-60cm).

The most familiar anthurium colours are pink (such as 'Avo-Anneke') or red (such as 'Fuego' and 'Brasil') with a yellow spadix, although other colours are increasing in production and popularity — white (such as 'Avo Jose') and orange (such as ('Favoriet'). The dark green, heart-shaped leaves are popular as cut foliage (see Chapter 3).

TIME TO BUY: The flowers should already be open.

AVAILABILITY: All year round.

VASE LIFE: Anthurium flowers are very hardy, and will last around 2 weeks before they begin to brown.

SPECIAL HOME CARE: Mist the flowers frequently with water. Keep away from excess cold, excess heat and draughts.

TRADE CARE: See Special Care for 'Tropical' Flowers, Chapter 7.

Handle anthuriums carefully as they bruise very easily. They are usually shipped individually secured to a tray, or surrounded by straw or paper to protect them.

ANTIRRHINUM
Snapdragon

FAMILY: Scrophulariaceae

BOTANICAL NAME: *Antirrhinum majus*

DESCRIPTION: The flowers, 1¼-1½in (3-4cm) long, are tubular with rounded upper and lower lips. Up to 15 flowers appear close together along the stem, which when cut measures up to 3ft (1m) in length. The flowers come in a large range of colours.

TIME TO BUY: When the lower 2-3 florets are open.

AVAILABILITY: Mainly spring and summer.

VASE LIFE: Up to 2 weeks.

SPECIAL HOME CARE: Frequent re-cutting of stem ends has proved effective in lengthening their vase life. Remove the top 2-3in (5-8cm) of the stem, in order to promote flowering of the rest of the buds, and to avoid stem curvature. Keep away from fruit, vegetables, dying flowers and excess heat.

TRADE CARE: Best kept at 36-41°F (1-5°C), although snapdragons can be held for up to 3 weeks as low as 32°F (0°C). Hold them in a vertical position, to avoid stem curvature, and keep in water and with light. Storage without water is not recommended, and prolonged exposure to darkness will result in washed-out colours.

They are sensitive to ethylene gas damage.

SUITABLE FOR DRYING

AQUILEGIA
Columbine

FAMILY: Ranunculaceae

BOTANICAL NAME: *Aquilegia hybrida*

DESCRIPTION: Terminal, bonnet-shaped flowers made up of five petals, each with its own protruding spur. The flowers are approximately 1¼-3in (3-8cm) long. Overall length, when cut, is no more than 20in (50cm). White, pink, yellow, blue and shades of purple varieties exist.

TIME TO BUY: When the flowers are starting to open.

AVAILABILITY: Summer.

VASE LIFE: 5-7 days.

TRADE CARE: Best kept at 36-41°F (2-5°C). Lower temperatures may cause discoloration of the petals. Place in water as soon as possible.

Aquilegia does not keep well.

ARACHNIS
Spider orchid

Arachnis flos-aeris

FAMILY: Orchidaceae

BOTANICAL NAME: *Arachnis flos-aeris*

DESCRIPTION: Small flowers with long, slender petals and sepals (usually spotted), each approximately

1½in (4cm) across, are borne along the end of a slender stem. The overall length, when cut, varies between 1-2 ft (30-60cm).

The main variety is 'Maggei Oei' (bronze).

TIME TO BUY: When approximately half of the flowers on the spike are open.

AVAILABILITY: All year round.

VASE LIFE: Up to 2 weeks.

SPECIAL HOME CARE: See Special Care for Orchids, Chapter 1.

TRADE CARE: See Special Care for 'Tropical' Flowers, Chapter 7.

ARANDA

Aranda

FAMILY: Orchidaceae

BOTANICAL NAME: *Aranda* species

DESCRIPTION: This is a cross between *Arachnis* and *Vanda*. It has the same characteristic long petals of arachnis, and the long-lasting qualities of vanda. The blooms, mainly pink, vary in size from 1½in (4cm) to up to 4in (10cm) across. There is an average of 8 blooms per spike, on a stem 1-2 ft (30-60cm) long.

The main varieties are 'Christine' (pink) of which no. 1 and no. 130 are the most common. 'Hilda Galistan', 'Norah', 'Peter Ewart' and 'Wendy Scott'

are also popular pink varieties. 'Kooi Choo' (red), 'Lam Chin' (yellow) and 'Peng Lee Yeoh' (purple) are less common.

TIME TO BUY: When at least half of the flowers on the spike are fully open.

AVAILABILITY: All year round.

VASE LIFE: Up to 2 weeks.

SPECIAL HOME CARE: See Special Care for Orchids, Chapter 1.

TRADE CARE: See Special Care for 'Tropical' Flowers, Chapter 7.

ARANTHERA

FAMILY: Orchidaceae

BOTANICAL NAME: *Aranthera* species

DESCRIPTION: Hybrid between *Arachnis* and *Renanthera*, these long-petalled, orchid flowers are approximately 1½-2½in (4-6cm) across. The slender stems bear an average of 8-10 blooms. The average overall length is 12-20in (30-50cm).

The most popular varieties are: 'James Storei' (red) and 'Anne Black' (red). Less common are 'Beatrice' (yellow) and *Limbeta storiei* (bronze).

TIME TO BUY: At least half the blooms on the spike should be fully open.

AVAILABILITY: All year round.

VASE LIFE: Up to 2 weeks.

SPECIAL HOME CARE: See Special Care for Orchids, Chapter 1.

TRADE CARE: See Special Care for 'Tropical' Flowers, Chapter 7.

ASCLEPIAS
Blood flower, Milkweed

FAMILY: Asclepiadaceae

BOTANICAL NAME: *Asclepias tuberosa*

DESCRIPTION: Round clusters of tiny, waxy, orange flowers at the end of stalks, which branch out from a single thick stem. The flowers are crown-like and are about ¼in (0.5cm) wide. The stems, when cut, are usually no more than 16in (40cm) long.

TIME TO BUY: When the majority of the flowers on the cluster are open.

AVAILABILITY: Summer.

VASE LIFE: Over 7 days, during which time the florets continue to open up. The problem is that the dying florets turn brown and do not fall off, so that after no more than 3 days, the overall effect is of a wilted flower head, even though the majority of the flowers may still be fresh.

SPECIAL HOME CARE: Keep away from draughts, excess heat and direct sunlight. Remove any brown florets.

TRADE CARE: Best kept at 36-41°F (2-5°C). Storage is not recommended.

ASCONCEDA

Asconceda

FAMILY: Orchidaceae

BOTANICAL NAME: *Asconceda* species

DESCRIPTION: Dendrobium-like orchid consisting of flowers, around 2 in (15 cm) across, with rounded petals. There are approximately 8-12 flowers on a stem. The overall length of the stem is usually 12-20 in (30-50 cm). The main colours are pink and red.

TIME TO BUY: At least half of the buds on the spray should be fully open.

AVAILABILITY: All year round.

VASE LIFE: Up to 2 weeks.

SPECIAL HOME CARE: See Special Care for Orchids, Chapter 1.

TRADE CARE: See Special Care for 'Tropical' Flowers, Chapter 7.

ASTER
Michaelmas daisy

For China aster, see Callistephus

FAMILY: Compositae

BOTANICAL NAME: *Aster novi-belgii*, *A. novae-angliae* and hybrids

DESCRIPTION: Michaelmas daisies are daisy-like flowers, ³/₄-3 in (2-8 cm) across, double or single, that come in a variety of colours, usually with a yellow centre. The flowers are borne at the end of stalks, that branch off a single stem. The stem length varies between 12-36 in (30-90 cm).

The main varieties are: 'Royal Velvet', 'Blue Gown' (lilac with yellow centre), 'White Ladies', 'White Climax' (white), 'Crimson Brocade' (red), 'Barr's Pink' (pink).

× *Solidaster luteus* is a hybrid between *Solidago* and *Aster*, and has tiny yellow flowers that appear in loose terminal clusters.

A. ericoides (September flower) has tiny, white, daisy-like flowers that appear in profusion on branched stems. Purple varieties also exist.

TIME TO BUY: When mature, i.e. with the majority of the flowers on the spray open. Cut too early, they will not open afterwards.

AVAILABILITY: End of summer to autumn.

VASE LIFE: Up to 10 days.

SPECIAL HOME CARE: Frequent re-cutting of the stems. Keep away from draughts and excess heat.

TRADE CARE: Best kept at 36-41°F (2-5°C). Place in water as soon as possible. Storage is not recommended.

ASTILBE

FAMILY: Saxifragaceae

BOTANICAL NAME: *Astilbe* species

DESCRIPTION: Minute flowers are borne in loose, pyramidal panicles, 12-16 in (30-40 cm) long, at the end of a slender stem, giving a feathery effect. The stem, when cut, averages 1½-2¼ ft (50-70 cm) in length.

The main varieties are pink, white and red, mostly from *A.* × *arendsii* but also from *A. simplicifolia*.

TIME TO BUY: When fully developed.

AVAILABILITY: Summer.

VASE LIFE: 1 week. The leaves tend to die off before the flowers.

SPECIAL HOME CARE: Astilbe stems 'bleed' when cut, so sear the end of the stem with a flame or immerse in boiling water for a few seconds.

TRADE CARE: Best kept at 36-41°F (2-5°C). Storage is not recommended.
SUITABLE FOR DRYING

ASTRANTIA
Masterwort

Astrantia major

FAMILY: Umbelliferae
BOTANICAL NAME: *Astrantia* species
DESCRIPTION: Tiny, star-shaped flowers measuring 1 in (2.5 cm) across, are borne in clusters. There are 6-8 clusters at the end of a stem that averages 20-24 in (50-60 cm) in length. The flowers are mainly in shades of red and pink, although some white varieties are also available.

The main varieties used for cut flowers are *A. major* (greenish-pink), and *A. carniolica* 'Rubra' (dark pink).

Astrantia has a strong, rather unpleasant smell.
TIME TO BUY: When the majority of the flowers on the cluster are open.
AVAILABILITY: Early summer.
VASE LIFE: 5-7 days.
TRADE CARE: Best kept at 36-41°F (2-5°C). Storage is not recommended.

BANKSIA

FAMILY: Proteaceae
BOTANICAL NAME: *Banksia* species
DESCRIPTION: Dense, terminal flower head from 4-10 in (10-25 cm) or more long, in red or yellow shades. The flower heads consist of a cone with numerous flowers, in the shape of a long or rounded bottle brush. They stand singly at the end of woody stems that are rarely more than 20 in (50 cm) long.

Banksias can be divided according to their shape (cup- or bottle-brush-shaped) and size (small, medium and large).
YELLOW: Cup-shaped such as *B. baxteri* and *B. speciosa* (small), *B. burdetti* and *B. victoriae* (medium). Bottle-brush-shaped such as *B. australis* and *B. attenuata* (small).
RED/ORANGE: Cup-shaped such as *B. spinulosa* and *B. speciosa* (small). Bottle-brush-shaped such as *B. coccinea* and *B. australis* (small) and *B. occidentalis* (large).
TIME TO BUY: When fully developed. Once cut, banksia do not continue to open.
AVAILABILITY: Different varieties are available at different times of the year, but mainly from January to May.
VASE LIFE: Approximately 2 weeks.
SPECIAL HOME CARE: Do not crush the stem ends; re-cut using secateurs or soften with boiling water.
TRADE CARE: Best kept at approximately 41°F (5°C) with high relative humidity. Can be kept dry for up to one week, then place in water.

Banksias can rot easily if they are slightly damp, so care should be taken to remove the lids from the boxes and place the boxes where there is good air circulation.
SUITABLE FOR DRYING

BELLFLOWER
Campanula

FAMILY: Campanulaceae
BOTANICAL NAME: *Campanula* species
DESCRIPTION: Blue or white open, bell-shaped flowers, ¾-1½ (2-4 cm) long, that are borne along and close to the stem. The stem usually reaches a height of 2-2½ ft (60-80 cm).

The main varieties are: *Campanula persicifolia*, with open, bell-shaped flowers on a spike; *C. pyramidalis*, with narrower, bell-shaped flowers on a spike; *C. glomerata*, with smaller, bell-shaped flowers forming a terminal cluster.
TIME TO BUY: When the first buds on the stem are clearly showing colour but have not yet opened. If bought when more than one flower is open, they will have only a short vase life, as they develop very quickly.
AVAILABILITY: Spring through to the end of the summer.
VASE LIFE: 5-7 days.
TRADE CARE: Best kept at 36-41°F (2-5°C). Place in water as soon as possible. Storage is not recommended.

BELLIS
Common daisy, English daisy

FAMILY: Compositae
BOTANICAL NAME: *Bellis perennis*
DESCRIPTION: The flowers, 1¼-2 in (3-5 cm) across, come in single forms with white petals surrounding a yellow centre, and in double forms consisting of a round densely-packed, pompon shape, in a variety of colours. The overall length, when cut, is no more than 10-14 in (25-35 cm).
TIME TO BUY: When the flowers have started to open.
AVAILABILITY: Spring and summer.
VASE LIFE: 5-7 days.
SPECIAL HOME CARE: Frequent stem re-cutting is advised as the stems are easily obstructed. Remove excess foliage.
TRADE CARE: Best kept at 36-41°F (2-5°C). Place in water as soon as possible. Storage is not recommended.

BORONIA

Boronia ledifolia

FAMILY: Rutaceae
BOTANICAL NAME: *Boronia ledifolia*
DESCRIPTION: Often confused with leptospermum with which boronia is not related. It has, like leptospermum, small waxy flowers that come in loose clusters. The flowers are mainly pink. The stem, when cut, is approximately 20 in (50 cm) long.
TIME TO BUY: The majority of the florets should be opening.
AVAILABILITY: All year.
VASE LIFE: 7-10 days.
SPECIAL HOME CARE: Avoid excess heat.
TRADE CARE: Best kept at 36-41°F (2-5°C). Storage is not recommended. Handling of the flowers should be kept to a minimum as the florets drop easily.

BOUVARDIA

FAMILY: Rubiaceae
BOTANICAL NAME: *Bouvardia longiflora* and hybrids.
DESCRIPTION: Small, tubular flowers with four spreading petals, forming a loose terminal cluster that is usually around 6 in (15 cm) wide. The overall length, when cut, varies from 20-24 in (50-70 cm).

The flowers are often fragrant, and are mainly red, pink or white, such as: 'Red King' (red), 'Sappho' (pink), 'Artemis' and 'Longiflora' (white).

TIME TO BUY: When the first 2-3 florets have started to open. White varieties are an exception and should be bought when the buds are showing colour but have not yet opened.

AVAILABILITY: Late spring to early winter.

VASE LIFE: 1 week (possibly up to 3 weeks).

SPECIAL HOME CARE: Bouvardia is very prone to water loss, so frequent re-cutting of the stem ends and the addition of flower food (if possible, the one produced specifically for bouvardia) will help ensure a steady flow of fresh water up to the flowers. The top bud is best removed upon arrival, as this will help the other flowers to develop. Removal of any excess foliage is also recommended.

Keep away from draughts, direct sunlight and excess heat.

TRADE CARE: Best kept at 36-41°F (2-5°C). Lower temperatures can cause frost damage and produce limp flowers that do not open up well. Place in water as soon as possible. Storage is not recommended.

BRODIAEA
Triteleia

FAMILY: Liliaceae

BOTANICAL NAME: *Triteleia laxa*

DESCRIPTION: Loose, terminal clusters formed by widely tubular flowers, each of which is 1½-2 in (4-5 cm) long. The stem length varies between 16-24 in (40-60 cm). The flowers are dark blue or violet.

B. laxa and *B.* 'Queen Fabiola' are both blue, the latter has larger flowers.

TIME TO BUY: A few blooms on the cluster should have already opened.

AVAILABILITY: Late spring to summer.

VASE LIFE: 2 weeks, during which time the flowers will continue to open up.

SPECIAL HOME CARE: When re-cutting the stem ends, remove the white lower section of the stem, which does not take in water well.

TRADE CARE: Best kept at 36-41°F (2-5°C). If the buds are very tight, keep at room temperature. In cooled conditions they can be held for up to 4 days dry, although it is recommended they be placed in water.

CALENDULA
English marigold, Pot marigold

FAMILY: Compositae

BOTANICAL NAME: *Calendula officinalis*

DESCRIPTION: Daisy-like, double flowers, 2½-4 in (6-10 cm) across, with bright yellow or orange petals and centre. The overall length, when cut, rarely exceeds 12-16 in (30-40 cm).

TIME TO BUY: The flowers should already be open.

AVAILABILITY: Spring and early summer.

VASE LIFE: 5-7 days.

SPECIAL HOME CARE: Remove excess foliage.

TRADE CARE: Best kept at 36-41°F (2-5°C). Place in water as soon as possible. Storage is not recommended.

CALLISTEPHUS
China aster

Callistephus chinensis

FAMILY: Compositae

BOTANICAL NAME: *Callistephus chinensis*

DESCRIPTION: Solitary, large, daisy-like flowers that come in a variety of shapes (mainly singles, doubles and spider-like), and in a variety of colours — mainly blue, lavender, various pinks and white. The flower size ranges from 2-4 in (5-10 cm). The stem length, when cut, also varies according to the variety, but is 2 ft (60 cm) long on average. The longest-lasting asters are the large-flowered, fully double strains.

Spider forms (such as 'Unicorn' (yellow)), single forms (such as 'Asterix' (purple with yellow centre)) and double forms (such as 'Ostrich Plume' (mauve)) are available as cut flowers.

TIME TO BUY: The flowers should just be starting to open.

AVAILABILITY: Late summer.

VASE LIFE: 5-7 days.

SPECIAL HOME CARE: Remove any excess foliage.

TRADE CARE: Best kept at 36-41°F (2-5°C). Place in water as soon as possible. Storage is not recommended.

CAMELLIA

Camellia japonica

FAMILY: Theaceae

BOTANICAL NAME: *Camellia japonica*

DESCRIPTION: Solitary waxy flowers, 2¾-6 in (7-15 cm) across, that come in white, pink, red, and multi-coloured, in single or double forms, that appear at the end of short branchlets, on long woody stems. They are fragrant.

There are many varieties of camellia, but the main ones used for cut flowers come from *C. japonica*.

TIME TO BUY: When the flowers are starting to open.

AVAILABILITY: Mainly spring.

VASE LIFE: Only 3-4 days, once cut.

SPECIAL HOME CARE: Camellias are very perishable, and need to be placed in water immediately and misted with water frequently.

TRADE CARE: Best kept at around 45°F (7°C), with a high humidity level. Lower temperatures can cause marking of the petals.

CARNATION
Dianthus

FAMILY: Caryophyllaceae

BOTANICAL NAME: *Dianthus* species

DESCRIPTION: Five-petalled double flowers that rise from a tubular calyx. The size of the stem varies according to the variety.

STANDARD CARNATIONS: Solitary flower, 2-3 in (5-8 cm) across, on a stem that averages 16-28 in (40-70 cm). The main colours are red, white, pink, yellow, orange, mauve and bi-coloured. Carnations can be tinted. These include the 'Sim' varieties, 'Mediterranean' varieties and hybrids of the two. Typical varieties include 'Scania' (red) and 'Rayo di Sole' (orange).

CHINESE, BUTTERFLY OR 'MIGNON' CARNATIONS: Solitary flower with frilled petals, 1¼-1½ in (3-4 cm) across, stem length 1-2 ft (30-60 cm). Available in purple, white, pink and red, but are mostly bi-coloured. A typical variety is 'Pulcino' (yellow).

MIDI CARNATIONS: Single flower head, with slightly frilled petals, ¾-1¼ in (2-3 cm) across, stem length 8-12 in (20-30 cm). Mainly bi-coloured, such as 'Sissi' (yellow with red edges).

SPRAY OR MINI CARNATIONS: 3-7 flowers per stem, the flowers are 1¼-1½ in (3-4 cm) across, stem length 16-24 in (40-60 cm). The main colours are red, pink, white, orange, mauve, yellow and bi-coloured. Typical varieties include 'Red Baron' (red), 'Silvery Pink' (pink) and 'Barbara' (pink).

MICRO CARNATIONS: 2-4 flowers per stem, flower size ½-¾ in (1.5-2 cm) across, stem length 12-16 in (30-40 cm). These are often called EOLO, after the variety of that name. The main colours are white, red, purple, yellow and bi-coloured.

DIANTHINI CARNATIONS: 2-4 flowers per stem, the flowers are less than ¾ in (2 cm) across and are edged with white, and the stems are 12-16 in (30-40 cm) in length. A typical variety is 'Sorentino' (pink).

PINKS: 1-3 opening flowers per stem, flowers ¾-1½in (2-4cm) across, stem length 8-16in (20-40cm). A quantity of unopened buds are usually left on the stem. The most popular single-flowered variety ('Doris') is light pink. Darker pink single forms, such as 'Christopher' and 'Joy', also exist. The variety 'Haytor' is double white.

TIME TO BUY: Before they are fully open.

Spray, micro and dianthini types: when the majority of the buds are showing colour, with a few of the buds half open.

Pinks: when only a few buds, that will open, are showing colour.

Standard, mignon and midi: when the buds are half open.

AVAILABILITY: All year round.

VASE LIFE: Up to 3 weeks.

SPECIAL HOME CARE: Keep away from ripe fruit, vegetables, diseased or damaged flowers, household fumes and heat — as these may speed wilting. Good air circulation is advisable.

TRADE CARE: Best kept at 36-41°F (2-5°C). Carnations can be held for up to one week dry, at 32-34°F (0-1°C). When storing carnations, make sure they are dry in the box, and that there is good air circulation and high humidity, or botrytis may develop.

Carnations are sensitive to even the smallest amount of ethylene gas, which can inhibit their development. Temperature control is, therefore, critical: temperatures above 47°F (8°C) can cause serious ethylene gas damage which may result in 'sleepiness' (shrivelling and browning of the petals) which can result in no flowers opening at all. Carnations should always be shipped pre-cooled.

Silver treatment has proved immensely effective, increasing vase life by up to 75 per cent.

Carnations are graded according to stem length, size of bloom, and, in the case of spray types, number of bloom buds per stem. As yet there is no world-wide standardisation of grades.

THE SPRAY VARIETIES ARE SUITABLE FOR DRYING

CARTHAMUS
Safflower

FAMILY: Compositae

BOTANICAL NAME: *Carthamus tinctorius*

DESCRIPTION: The flowers are ¾-1¼in (2-3cm) across, and consist of a green, globular centre, from which thin orange petals appear. The flowers appear at the end of short branchlets that come off a single stem. The stem length, when cut, is approximately 20-28in (50-70cm).

TIME TO BUY: When the majority of the buds on the stem have broken and are clearly showing the petals. Once cut, carthamus buds do not open unless they are showing good colour.

AVAILABILITY: Summer.

VASE LIFE: Over 1 week, although the foliage dries up before the flowers do.

SPECIAL HOME CARE: Avoid draughts and excess heat, that may take up humidity.

TRADE CARE: Best kept at 36-39°F (2-4°C). Carthamus are long-lasting flowers, but the foliage dries up quickly, which makes them unsuitable for any length of storage.

SUITABLE FOR DRYING

CATANANCHE
Cupid's dart

Catananche caerulea

FAMILY: Compositae

BOTANICAL NAME: *Catananche caerulea*

DESCRIPTION: Small flowers, 1½in (4cm) across, similar in shape to cornflowers, with papery bracts that appear singly at the end of wiry stems that are usually 16-24 in (40-60 cm) long. The most common varieties come in shades of blue and purple, although some white and bi-coloured (white-blue) varieties exist.

TIME TO BUY: The flowers should be starting to open.

AVAILABILITY: Summer.

VASE LIFE: 5-7 days.

TRADE CARE: Best kept at 36-41°F (2-5°C). Place in water as soon as possible. Storage is not recommended.

SUITABLE FOR DRYING

CATTLEYA

Cattleya loddigesii

FAMILY: Orchidaceae

BOTANICAL NAME: *Cattleya* hybrid

DESCRIPTION: The flowers measure 2¾-5 in (7-12 cm) across, and consist of three colourful sepals, large side petals and a broad, tongue-shaped lip that is usually frilled or fringed. One or more flowers appear at the end of a stem that is usually no more than 20 in (50 cm) in length. This is usually considered the queen of all orchids because of its perfect shape.

The main varieties used for cut flower production are hybrids, that come in shades of pink, lavender, yellow and white.

TIME TO BUY: When the flowers are open.

AVAILABILITY: All year round.

VASE LIFE: Up to 2 weeks.

SPECIAL HOME CARE: See Special Care for Orchids, Chapter 1.

TRADE CARE: See Special Care for 'Tropical' Flowers, Chapter 7.

CELOSIA
Cockscomb, Prince of Wales feather

FAMILY: Amaranthaceae

BOTANICAL NAME: *Celosia argentea*

DESCRIPTION: There are two types of Celosia:

C. *plumosa* (known as Prince of Wales feather) consists of a feathery flower plume, 2½-6 in (6-15 cm) high, that is red or yellow. The flower heads appear at the end of stems that average 24-28 in (60-70 cm) in length.

C. *christata* (known as cockscomb) consists of a compact crested head, 2¾-5 in (7-12 cm) across, of red, yellow or orange flowers. The flower head appears at the end of a stem that can vary from 12 in (30 cm) to over 28 in (70 cm) in length.

TIME TO BUY: When fully developed.

AVAILABILITY: Late summer and autumn.

VASE LIFE: 5-6 days.

SPECIAL HOME CARE: The crested variety is longer-lasting than the plumed one, but in both cases the foliage tends to go limp and rot very quickly, so is best removed as it wilts. Frequent changing of water is recommended.

TRADE CARE: Best kept between 36-41°F (2-5°C). Storage is not recommended.

SUITABLE FOR DRYING

CENTAUREA
Bachelor's button, Cornflower

FAMILY: Compositae

BOTANICAL NAME: *Centaurea cyanus*, *C. macrocephela*

DESCRIPTION: There are two types of centaurea that are commonly used as cut flowers:

C. *cyanus* (known as bachelor's button or cornflower), consists of small, thistle-like flowers that are ¾-1½ in (2-4 cm) across, mainly blue, but also found in pink, red, purple and white. They appear at the end of small branchlets, forming a spray. The stem

length is usually no more than 16-20 in (40-50 cm). C. *macrocephala* is a larger flower, 2¾-4 in (7-10 cm) that is yellow, and stands singly at the end of a stout stem, usually over 20 in (50 cm) in length.
TIME TO BUY: When the flowers are only half open.
AVAILABILITY: Mainly late spring to early summer.
VASE LIFE: 5-7 days.
TRADE CARE: Best kept at 36-41°F (2-5°C). At these temperatures they can be held for 2-3 days in water.
SUITABLE FOR DRYING

CHAMAELAUCIUM
Tea-tree, Waxflower

Chamaelaucium uncinatum

Chamaelaucium is very similar to leptospermum, and of the same family. Since they are often confused, in the following notes they have been treated together.

In the USA, leptospermum is generally known as pink tea tree or waxplant (specifically, geralton waxplant). Waxflower is also another name for stephanotis and, to add to the confusion, waxplant is also the name for *Hoya bella*.
FAMILY: Myrtaceae
BOTANICAL NAME: *Leptospermum scoparium, Chamaelaucium uncinatum*
DESCRIPTION: Star-shaped, white or pink flowers,

½ in (1 cm) wide, that are single or double, occur in profusion on a shrub or small tree. When cut, the stem is no more than 16-20 in (40-50 cm) long.
TIME TO BUY: When the majority of the flowers have begun to open.
AVAILABILITY: Winter and spring.
VASE LIFE: Around 10 days.
TRADE CARE: Best kept cooled at 36-41°F (2-5°C), ideally, 39°F (4°C). At these temperatures, they can be held without water for up to 2 days, and up to 5 days in water.
SUITABLE FOR DRYING

CHEIRANTHUS
Wallflower

Cheiranthus cheiri

FAMILY: Cruciferae
BOTANICAL NAME: *Cheiranthus cheiri*
DESCRIPTION: The cross-shaped flowers, with rounded, oblong petals, are approximately 1 in (2.5 cm) wide, and appear in clusters at the end of stems that are no more than 12-16 in (30-40 cm) in length. The flowers are orange, red, yellow, cream and purple.
TIME TO BUY: When only a few of the blooms have opened.

AVAILABILITY: Spring.

VASE LIFE: 4-6 days.

SPECIAL HOME CARE: Place in good light (although away from direct sunlight).

TRADE CARE: Best kept at 36-41°F (2-5°C). Storage is not recommended.

CHELONE
Turtle head

Chelone obliqua

FAMILY: Scrophulariaceae

BOTANICAL NAME: *Chelone obliqua*

DESCRIPTION: Snapdragon-like, pink flowers, 1 in (2.5 cm) long, appear in a terminal, dense cluster at the end of a thick stem. The stem length is usually 18-22 in (45-55 cm).

TIME TO BUY: When only 2-3 flowers on the spike have started to open.

AVAILABILITY: Late summer to autumn.

VASE LIFE: 1 week.

TRADE CARE: Best kept at 36-41°F (2-5°C). At these temperatures they can be held for 4-6 days in water. Storage without water is not recommended. Prolonged storage will result in petal drop.

CHRYSANTHEMUM
Florist's chrysanthemum

FAMILY: Compositae

BOTANICAL NAME: *Chrysanthemum* species

DESCRIPTION: Chrysanthemums are divided into spray types (with many flowers per stem) and disbudded types (one flower per stem). These in turn are divided according to their shape, e.g.:

SPRAY CHRYSANTHEMUM (also known as pompon chrysanthemums or sprays): The flowers appear at the end of branchlets that are borne off a single stem. There are 3-7 flower heads per stem. The overall length when cut varies between 20-32 in (50-80 cm). The most popular flower forms are:

Spider: the petals are tubular and thread-like. The main varieties are 'Westland' and 'Spider', which both come in white, yellow and mauve.

Single: Up to five rows of petals surrounding a clearly visible, central disc. A popular variety is 'Horim', which is available in petal colours of pink, white, purple, orange, yellow and bronze, often with a yellow centre.

Decorative or semi-double: similar to the single types, but the central disc is larger, and consists of tubular florets that form a raised cushion, and are often the same colour as the surrounding petals. The most popular of this group is the variety 'Refour' (white, yellow and, sometimes, pink).

These are often also classified as anemone types, and include varieties such as 'Penny Lane' (pink) and 'Daymark' (white with a yellow centre).

Pompon or buttons: blooms with close, firm petals, forming a tight globe. Includes white or yellow varieties, such as 'Statesman' (yellow).

Decorative, double or cushion: rayed flowers, that form a full, informal shape. They come in bronze, pink, yellow, white and mauve. 'Polaris' (yellow or white) is one of the most popular varieties.

STANDARD OR SINGLE CHRYSANTHEMUMS (also known as blooms, disbudded chrysanthemums or mums): A single flower head, over 4 in (10 cm) across, appears at the end of a single stem that is usually 20-24 in (50-60 cm) long. The most popular flower forms are:

Incurved: the bloom shape is that of a perfect globe, such as 'Rivalry' (yellow) and 'Shoesmith' (yellow or white).

Reflexed: similar to the incurved, but less formal and globose, such as 'Tom Pierce' (bronze).

Tubular: the petals are thread-like and tubular. Tubular types include: spider, with long thin petals; fugi, with shorter petals; quill, with shorter petals in the centre of the flower; and spoon, with flattened outer rays. All these types come mainly in yellow and white.

Single: a single row of petals surrounding a central disc, such as 'Cremon' (white petals, yellow centre).

The single and tubular varieties are generally smaller than the incurved and reflexed varieties.

TIME TO BUY: Spray types: when most of the florets have already opened; standard or single types: the flower head should be half or fully open.

Chrysanthemums are not usually bought in the bud stage. If they are, use of a bud opening solution will be necessary, otherwise the flowers will not open up at all.

AVAILABILITY: All year round.

VASE LIFE: Chrysanthemums are very long-lasting flowers, with a vase life of 10 days or more.

SPECIAL HOME CARE: The foliage usually deteriorates before the flowers. Remove the foliage as it dies, as this will make the flowers last longer. Re-cut, rather than crush or split, the stem ends, making sure to remove the woodier part of the stem that does not take in water easily. The use of flower food, and frequent re-cutting of the stem ends are important, since chrysanthemums are prone to stem blockage, caused by bacterial build-up in the water.

TRADE CARE: Chrysanthemums should be kept cooled at between 36-41°F (2-5°C), and as much as 39-47°F (4-8°C) is recommended. Chrysanthemums in unpacked boxes can be held as low as 32-34°F (0-2°C). At these temperatures they can be held dry for up to one week, and in water for up to 2 weeks. When keeping chrysanthemums for any amount of time, keep the light on in the cold room, to ensure proper development of the flowers. High humidity, low temperature and good air circulation are all important when storing these flowers.

Although not overly sensitive to ethylene gas damage, chrysanthemums emit a large amount of this gas, and so should be kept separate from carnations, antirrhinums, orchids and other ethylene gas sensitive flowers, unless they are all under cooled conditions.

SMALL-HEADED FLOWERS ARE SUITABLE FOR DRYING

CHRYSANTHEMUM FRUTESCENS
Marguerite, Boston daisy

Chrysanthemum frutescens

FAMILY: Compositae

DESCRIPTION: Daisy-like flower, 1¼-2¾in (3-7cm) across, that consists of a yellow centre surrounded by white, yellow or pink petals. The stem length is 10-16in (25-40cm). The flowers are often tinted.

TIME TO BUY: When the majority of the flowers have already opened.

AVAILABILITY: Mainly summer.

VASE LIFE: Up to 10 days.

TRADE CARE: Best kept at 36-41°F (2-5°C). At these temperatures they can be held in water for 4-6 days.

CHRYSANTHEMUM MAXIMUM
Shasta daisy

Chrysanthemum maximum

FAMILY: Compositae
DESCRIPTION: White petals surround a yellow centre. The flower is 2-3 in (5-8 cm) across in single forms, and 4 in (10 cm) across in double forms. The stem length is 16 in (40 cm) or more. The flowers are sometimes tinted.
TIME TO BUY: When fully developed.
AVAILABILITY: Mainly spring and early summer.
VASE LIFE: Over 1 week.
TRADE CARE: Best kept at 36-41°F (2-5°C). In these conditions, they can be held for up to 5 days in water.

CHRYSANTHEMUM PARTHENIUM
Matricaria, Capensis, Feverfew

FAMILY: Compositae
DESCRIPTION: Small flowers, either daisy-like with white petals surrounding a yellow centre, or white pompon-like, appear in quantities on branched stems that vary between 20-28 in (50-70 cm) in length.
TIME TO BUY: The flower should be starting to open.
AVAILABILITY: Summer.

VASE LIFE: Over 1 week.
TRADE CARE: Best kept at 36-41°F (2-5°C). In these conditions they can be held for up to 3-4 days in water.

CHRYSANTHEMUM SEGETUM
Corn marigold

FAMILY: Compositae
DESCRIPTION: Single flowers, usually 1 in (2.5 cm) across, with yellow petals surrounding a yellow or brown disc. The stem length is no more than 12-16 in (30-40 cm).
TIME TO BUY: When already opening.
AVAILABILITY: Early summer.
VASE LIFE: Over 1 week.
TRADE CARE: Best kept at 36-41°F (2-5°C). In these conditions, they can be held for 2-4 days in water.

CINERARIA

Cineraria cruenta stellata

FAMILY: Compositae
BOTANICAL NAME: *Cineraria* species
DESCRIPTION: The single or double, daisy-like flowers are up to 2¾ in (7 cm) across, and come in a large variety of colours, with bi-coloured petals. The

stem length when cut averages 14 in (35 cm). Stellata types have star-like, one-coloured petals and there are also single and double forms with broader bi-coloured petals.

TIME TO BUY: When the flowers have started to open.

AVAILABILITY: Winter and spring.

VASE LIFE: Approximately 1 week.

TRADE CARE: Best kept at 36-41°F (2-5°C). Storage is not recommended.

CIRSIUM
Cnicus

FAMILY: Compositae

BOTANICAL NAME: *Cirsium rivulare*

DESCRIPTION: Small, thistle-like flowers, ¾-1¼ in (2-3 cm) across, appear in terminal clusters on stems that vary in height. The flowers come mainly in red and purple, rarely in yellow and white.

TIME TO BUY: When the flowers are open.

AVAILABILITY: All year round.

VASE LIFE: Approximately 1 week.

TRADE CARE: Best kept at 36-41°F (2-5°C). Storage is not recommended.

CLARKIA

Clarkia elegans

Clarkia is sometimes listed under godetia, but it is a different flower although belonging to the same family.

FAMILY: Onagraceae

BOTANICAL NAME: *Clarkia elegans*

DESCRIPTION: Double or semi-double flowers, 1½-2½ in (4-6 cm) across, that appear on a terminal spike. The flowers are white, pink, lavender, purple, red, salmon or orange. The overall length, when cut, is 16-20 in (40-50 cm).

TIME TO BUY: When only a few flowers on the spike have opened.

AVAILABILITY: Summer to autumn.

VASE LIFE: 5-7 days.

TRADE CARE: Best kept at over 47°F (8°C). Lower temperatures can cause frost damage; temperatures above 59°F (15°C) can cause premature wilting. They should not be held for more than 2-3 days without water. Once in water, they will start to open up immediately.

CLEMATIS

Clematis integrifolia

FAMILY: Ranunculaceae

BOTANICAL NAME: *Clematis* species

DESCRIPTION: The flowers are flat, bell- or cup-shaped, measure around 1¼-2 in (3-5 cm) across, and come in a variety of colours, although white, and shades of pink and purple, are the most common. The stem length is approximately 10-16 in (25-40 cm). Popular types include C. *alpina*, C. *armandii*, C. *integrifolia*, C. *macrocpetala*, C. *montana*, C. *orientalis* and C. *tangutica*.

TIME TO BUY: When the petals are starting to open out.

AVAILABILITY: Spring and summer.

VASE LIFE: Approximately 5 days.

SPECIAL HOME CARE: Avoid direct sunlight, draughts and excess heat as these flowers lose moisture easily.

TRADE CARE: Best kept at 45-47°F (7-8°C), although normal cold room temperatures, 34-41°F (1-5°C), will not harm the flowers. In cold temperatures, the flowers will close up, but once they are placed at room temperature they will open up. Clematis do not last at all well without water.

CLIVIA

Clivia miniata

The name of clivia causes some confusion, since it is sometimes used to refer to Kaffir lily (Schizostylis).

FAMILY: Amaryllidaceae

BOTANICAL NAME: *Clivia* species

DESCRIPTION: At the end of a stout, short stem, there appears a cluster of 6-10 flowers. The flowers measure 1¼-2 in (3-5 cm) across, are trumpet-shaped, and usually orange. The overall length when cut is no more than 10 in (25 cm). Popular types include C. *miniata* and C. *nobilis*. Some hybrids have flowers in white, and shades of salmon, red or yellow.

TIME TO BUY: When the first flowers on the cluster have started to open.

AVAILABILITY: Spring.

VASE LIFE: Up to 2 weeks, during which time the buds will continue to open up.

TRADE CARE: Best kept at 41-47°F (5-8°C). Lower temperatures may cause frost damage, resulting in discoloration of the petals, and non-opening of buds. They can be held for up to 4-6 days without water. Once in water they will begin to open up.

COREOPSIS

Coreopsis tinctoria

Sometimes listed as calliopsis.

FAMILY: Compositae

BOTANICAL NAME: *Coreopsis* species

DESCRIPTION: Daisy-like flowers, 1-2 in (2.5-5 cm) across, consist of yellow petals surrounding a yellow

or orange centre. The stem length is 16-20in (40-50cm). Main types used as cut flowers include C. *grandiflora* and C. *verticillata*.
AVAILABILITY: Spring and summer.
TIME TO BUY: The flowers should be fully developed.
VASE LIFE: Approximately 1 week.
TRADE CARE: Best kept at 36-41°F (2-5°C). Place in water as soon as possible. Storage is not recommended.

COSMEA
Cosmos

Cosmos sulphureus

FAMILY: Compositae
BOTANICAL NAME: *Cosmos*
DESCRIPTION: Single flowers, up to 4in (10cm) across, consisting of a single row of petals surrounding a yellow centre. The petals are white, yellow, and shades of red and pink. The stem length is usually 16-20in (40-50cm).
TIME TO BUY: The petals should have opened up, but not yet be lying flat.
AVAILABILITY: Summer.
VASE LIFE: 4-6 days.
SPECIAL HOME CARE: Keep away from draughts, heat and direct sunshine.

TRADE CARE: Best kept at 36-41°F (2-5°C). Place in water as soon as possible. Storage is not recommended.

CROCOSMIA
Montbretia

These flowers are closely related to tritonia, with which they are often confused.
FAMILY: Iridaceae
BOTANICAL NAME: *Crocosmia* × *crocosmiiflora* (also known as *Montbretia crocosmiiflora*)
DESCRIPTION: Trumpet-shaped flowers, 1½in (4cm) long, in shades ranging from orange to deep red, that appear in double ranks along the end of the stem. The overall length when cut is 20-28in (50-70cm).
TIME TO BUY: The first few buds on the stem should be showing colour but not yet have opened.
AVAILABILITY: Summer.
VASE LIFE: 7-10 days.
SPECIAL HOME CARE: Keep away from fruit, vegetables, dying flowers and excess heat, as these can cause premature wilting.
TRADE CARE: Best kept at 34-37°F (1-3°C). Crocosmia can be kept in controlled conditions for up to 4-5 days without water, although placing in water immediately is recommended. They are sensitive to ethylene gas damage.

CYCLAMEN

FAMILY: Primulaceae
BOTANICAL NAME: *Cyclamen* species
DESCRIPTION: There are many varieties of flower forms, all basically with sharply reflexed petals. The main colours are in shades of pink, although white varieties are also plentiful. The stem length is no more than 8in (20cm) long. Due to its short stem, cyclamen is usually sold as a pot plant and not as a cut flower, in spite of its long-lasting qualities.
TIME TO BUY: The flowers should be starting to open.
AVAILABILITY: Mainly winter.
VASE LIFE: One week to 10 days.
SPECIAL HOME CARE: Sear the end of the stem with a flame or immerse in boiling water for a few seconds, in order to stop 'bleeding' that can cause premature wilting.
TRADE CARE: Best kept at 36-41°F (2-5°C). Storage is not recommended.

CYMBIDIUM

FAMILY: Orchidaceae
BOTANICAL NAME: *Cymbidium* hybrids
DESCRIPTION: Spray of orchid flowers on an erect stem. Cymbidiums can be divided into:
CYMBIDIUMS OR STANDARD CYMBIDIUMS: On a stem that is usually 20-24 in (50-60 cm) long, there is an average of 8-12 flowers, each of which measures 2-3 in (5-8 cm) across. These are sold on the stem (price is usually quoted per bloom, not stem) or individually packed in a box. The main colours are yellow-green, red-orange, salmon and white-cream.
MINI CYMBIDIUMS: On a spray usually 16-20 in (40-50 cm) long, there are up to 20 flowers. The flowers measure 2-3 in (5-8 cm) across and come in yellow-green, white-cream, shades of red, brown, pink, orange and peach.
TIME TO BUY: Most of the flowers on the spike should have opened, with the top bud just starting to open.
AVAILABILITY: Mainly winter.
VASE LIFE: Up to 2 weeks, as long as a good flow of water is maintained. They are shipped with a water vial at the end of the stem.
SPECIAL HOME CARE: Remove the water vial before re-cutting the stem, and place in fresh water with flower food. Frequent misting with water will keep the moisture level high.
TRADE CARE: Best kept at 39-45°F (4-7°C). Cymbidiums are one of the few orchids that do not suffer frost damage when exposed to temperatures as low as 36°F (2°C). Avoid excess heat and draughts as these may dehydrate the flowers. Remove the water vial and replace with fresh water within 5 days of shipping.

CYNARA
Globe Artichoke

Cynara scolymus

FAMILY: Compositae
BOTANICAL NAME: *Cynara scolymus*
DESCRIPTION: Tight green, overlapping bracts form a rounded head that measures up to 2 in (5 cm) across, from which small purple flowers emerge. The flower head stands singly at the end of the stem, which is usually cut to around 20-24 in (50-60 cm).
TIME TO BUY: As soon as the buds are showing colour.
VASE LIFE: 1 week to 10 days.
SPECIAL HOME CARE: Frequent re-cutting of the stems and the addition of flower food will help reduce the yellowing of the leaves.
TRADE CARE: Best kept at 34-41°F (1-5°C). Storage is not recommended.

CYPRIPEDIUM
Paphiopedilum, Slipper orchid, Lady's slipper

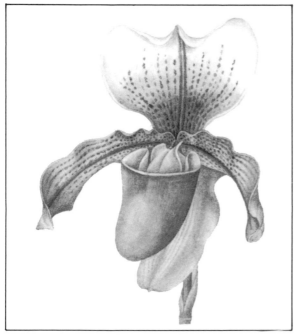

Paphiopedilum hybrid

FAMILY: Orchidaceae
BOTANICAL NAME: *Paphiopedilum*
DESCRIPTION: 1-2 small flowers, 1-2 in (2.5-5 cm) across, each with a protruding lip that makes them look similar to a slipper. The stem length is usually not more than 10 in (25 cm).

The main varieties are hybrids, mostly in white and shades of green, yellow and brownish-red.
TIME TO BUY: When the flowers are open.
AVAILABILITY: Mainly winter.
VASE LIFE: Up to 10 days.
SPECIAL HOME CARE: Remove the water vial before re-cutting the stem, and place in water with flower food. Frequent misting with water will help maintain a high level of humidity.
TRADE CARE: Best kept at 39-45°F (4-7°C). Cypripediums are among the few orchids that do not suffer frost damage when exposed to temperatures as low as 36°F (2°C). Avoid excess heat and draughts as these may dehydrate the flowers. Remove water vial and replace with fresh water within 5 days of shipping.

DAHLIA

FAMILY: Compositae
BOTANICAL NAME: *Dahlia* hybrids
DESCRIPTION: Dahlias vary in shape and size, and most colours, except blue, are available. In most types, the blooms vary in size between 4-6 in (10-15 cm) in diameter, although decorative, ball and cactus types can reach 10 in (25 cm) or more in diameter. The stem length reaches up to 2 ft (60 cm). The most popular flower types are:
SINGLE: A single row of petals surrounds a central disc, such as 'Sion' (bronze) and 'Orangeade' (orange).
ANEMONE: A double row of petals surrounds a centre that consists of a raised cushion of short petals, such as 'Bridesmaid' (white with a yellow centre), and 'Lucy' (purple with a yellow centre).
COLLERETTE: A single row of petals, with a row of shorter petals on top (called a collar), all surrounding a central disc. Varieties include 'Can Can' (pink outer row of petals, cream-coloured collar and a yellow centre).
PAEONY-FLOWERING: A double row of petals surrounds a central disc, such as 'Orange Flora' (orange).
DECORATIVE: Fully double, with a central, nearly invisible disc, such as 'Betty Russell' (yellow).
BALL: The petals are shaped into a perfect globe, or a globe that is flattened on top. Varieties include 'Nina Chester' (white).
CACTUS: Semi-double, with pointed ray florets, such as 'Authority' (yellow).
TIME TO BUY: When starting to open.
AVAILABILITY: Late summer and early autumn.
VASE LIFE: 5-8 days.
TRADE CARE: Best kept at 36-41°F (2-5°C). Place in water as soon as possible. Storage is not recommended.
SUITABLE FOR DRYING

DELPHINIUM

FAMILY: Ranunculaceae
BOTANICAL NAME: *Delphinium* species
DESCRIPTION: The flowers are 1/4-1/2 in (0.5-1.5 cm) across, cup-shaped, and appear in an 8-10 in (20-25 cm) long spike, at the end of a long (usually over 28 in (70 cm)) stem.

There are two distinct types used as cut flowers, usually referred to as larkspur and delphinium.
LARKSPUR (*Delphinium consolida*) is an annual, with

finely divided leaves, giving a fern-like appearance. Comes in shades of blue, lilac, pink and white. *D. ajacis* is a more dainty version.

This plant is poisonous.

DELPHINIUM (mainly derived from *D. elatum*) is a perennial, with shorter stems and, usually, blue or purple flowers.

WHEN TO BUY: When the majority of the lower flowers on the spike have opened.

AVAILABILITY: Spring and summer.

VASE LIFE: Approximately 1 week. Re-cutting of stem ends and addition of flower food will help reduce flower drop, to which this flower is prone, and will encourage proper opening of the flower buds. Keep away from fruit, vegetables, drying flowers and excess heat, which can encourage premature wilting.

TRADE CARE: Best kept cooled at 36-41°F (2-5°C). Place in water as soon as possible. Storage is not recommended. They are sensitive to ethylene gas damage.

MOST VARIETIES (especially larkspur) ARE SUITABLE FOR DRYING

DENDROBIUM

FAMILY: Orchidiaceae
BOTANICAL NAME: *Dendrobium phalaenopsis*
DESCRIPTION: These small, ¾-1¼in (2-3cm) flowers have sepals of equal length, and appear on spikes, up to 15 flowers per spike. The stems, when cut, are 12-20in (30-50cm) in length.

There are more than 900 types of dendrobiums, but only a few of them are common as cut flowers. The most popular are 'Madame Pompadour' (purple), 'Walter Omae' (white) and 'Caesar' (white-pinkish). True yellow and green varieties exist, and white varieties are often tinted.

TIME TO BUY: When the majority of the flowers on the stem have already opened, and only the very top flowers are in bud. Once cut, dendrobium buds rarely open.

AVAILABILITY: All year round.

VASE LIFE: Up to 3 weeks.

SPECIAL HOME CARE: See Special Care for Orchids, Chapter 1.

TRADE CARE: See Special Care for 'Tropical' Flowers, Chapter 7.

DIDISCUS
Laceflower

Trachymene caerulea

FAMILY: Umbelliferae
BOTANICAL NAME: The correct name is now *Trachymene caerulea*.
DESCRIPTION: The 12-16in (30-40cm) long stems carry 1½-2in (4-5cm) wide umbels of fragrant, lavender, rounded flowers.
TIME TO BUY: The flowers should be open.
AVAILABILITY: Summer.
VASE LIFE: 5-7 days.
TRADE CARE: Best kept at 36-41°F (2-5°C). Place in water as soon as possible. Storage is not recommended.

DIGITALIS
Foxglove

FAMILY: Scrophulariaceae
BOTANICAL NAME: *Digitalis purpurea*
DESCRIPTION: Long spikes, densely packed with large (2 in, 5 cm long) flowers, all facing one way, come on long stems, usually over 28 in (70 cm) in length. The main colour is pink, but yellow, white, red and purple varieties are also available.

All parts of the plant are poisonous.
TIME TO BUY: When only the lower florets on the spike are starting to open.
AVAILABILITY: Summer.
VASE LIFE: Over 2 weeks, during which time the florets will continue to open.
SPECIAL HOME CARE:

Since the flowers take time in opening, it is normal for the lower florets to wilt by the time the top ones are starting to develop. The wilted flowers should be removed.

Digitalis responds very favourably to frequent re-cutting of the stem ends, as their stems are prone to blockage.

Keep away from fruit, vegetables, excess heat and any decaying flowers.
TRADE CARE: Best kept at 34-36°F (1-2°C). Can be held for up to 5 days in this condition, but it is recommended they be placed in water as soon as possible. They are susceptible to ethylene gas damage.

DILL

FAMILY: Umbelliferae
BOTANICAL NAME: *Anethum graveolens* (also listed as *Peucedanum graveolens*)
DESCRIPTION: Tiny, starry, greenish-yellow or white flowers are borne in umbels at the end of thin stems, that branch from the top of a slender stem, giving a loose fan effect. The stems, when cut, reach approximately 2 ft (60 cm) in length.
TIME TO BUY: When the flowers are open.
AVAILABILITY: Summer.
VASE LIFE: 7-10 days.
TRADE CARE: Best kept at 36-41°F (2-5°C). Place in water as soon as possible.

DIMORPHOTHECA
Cape marigold, African daisy, Star of the Veldt

Dimorphotheca barberiae

FAMILY: Compositae
BOTANICAL NAME: *Dimorphotheca aurantiaca*
DESCRIPTION: Daisy-like flowers, 2 in (5 cm) across, consist of a centre, usually dark, surrounded by petals that are usually orange (*D. aurantica*), although yellow and white are also available, such as 'Glistening White' (white) and 'Las Vegas' (pastel colours). The stems, when cut, are usually no more than 16 in (40 cm) in length.
TIME TO BUY: The flowers should already be open.
AVAILABILITY: Mainly summer.
VASE LIFE: 5-7 days.
TRADE CARE: Best kept at 36-41°F (2-5°C). The flowers often arrive limp, but once they are placed in water they will revive. Storage is not recommended.

DORONICUM
Leopard's bane

Doronicum grandiflorum

FAMILY: Compositae
BOTANICAL NAME: *Doronicum* species
DESCRIPTION: Daisy-like, yellow flowers, 2-2½in (5-6cm) across, consist of a single row of petals surrounding a yellow centre. The stems, when cut, are over 1ft (30-40cm) long.
TIME TO BUY: When the flowers have opened.
AVAILABILITY: Spring and early summer.
VASE LIFE: Approximately 5 days.
TRADE CARE: Best kept at 36-41°F (2-5°C). Place in water as soon as possible. Storage is not recommended.

DRYANDRA

Dryandra polycephala

FAMILY: Proteaceae
BOTANICAL NAME: *Dryandra* species
DESCRIPTION: Orange or yellow, small (½in, 2cm across) flowers, usually carried in dense heads. The flowers are brittle, and appear on stems that are usually 20in (50cm) when cut.

The main species are: *D. formosa* (showy dryandra), terminal, solitary, yellow flower heads; *D. polysephala* (golden dryandra), yellow flowers that appear close to and along the length of the stem; *D. stupposa* (yellow dryandra), large terminal, solitary, yellow flower head.
TIME TO BUY: The flowers should be fully developed; once cut they do not continue to open.
AVAILABILITY: All year round, depending on the variety.
VASE LIFE: 2-3 weeks.
TRADE CARE: Best kept at 36-41°F (2-5°C). In these conditions, they can be held without water for up to 4-5 days.
SUITABLE FOR DRYING

ECHINOPS
Globe thistle

FAMILY: Compositae
BOTANICAL NAME: *Echinops ritro*
DESCRIPTION: Spherical, thistle-like flowers appear at the end of branching stems. The most common varieties are blue, and have a metallic lustre. The overall length, when cut, is usually over 28 in (70 cm).

Large varieties, up to 2 in (5 cm), include *E. ritro* (steely blue), 'Taplow Blue' (soft blue) and 'Blue Globe' (blue). Other varieties, with smaller blue heads, are also popular but not as common, such as the richly-coloured 'Veitch's Blue'.
TIME TO BUY: Best bought when a quarter of the blooms are open.
AVAILABILITY: Summer and early autumn.
VASE LIFE: Approximately 10 days.
TRADE CARE: Best kept at 36-41°F (2-5°C). At these temperatures they can be held dry for 3-4 days, but it is recommended they be placed in water as soon as possible as the foliage dries up.
SUITABLE FOR DRYING

EPIDENDRUM

Epidendrum fragrans

FAMILY: Orchidaceae
BOTANICAL NAME: *Epidendrum* species
DESCRIPTION: Spray with 12 or more orchid flowers, each approximately 4 in (10 cm) across, that have a lip which is longer than the petals and sepals. They come in a variety of colours, usually bi-coloured. The stem, when cut, is 20-24 in (50-60 cm) long.
TIME TO BUY: When the majority of the flowers on the stem have opened. The last few buds usually never open at all.
AVAILABILITY: All year round.
VASE LIFE: Up to 2 weeks.
SPECIAL HOME CARE: See Special Care for Orchids, Chapter 1.
TRADE CARE: See Special Care for 'Tropical Flowers', Chapter 7.

EREMURUS
Foxtail lily, Desert candle

FAMILY: Liliaceae
BOTANICAL NAME: *Eremurus stenophyllus, E. robustus* and hybrids
DESCRIPTION: Long spikes, bearing small, star-shaped flowers, appear at the end of a long (up to 3 ft, 1 m) stem. The flowers are usually yellow, although there are also white, cream, orange and pink varieties.
TIME TO BUY: When only the bottom half of the flowers on the spike have opened.
AVAILABILITY: Summer.
VASE LIFE: Approximately 1 week, during which time new florets will open and the bottom flowers will wilt.
SPECIAL HOME CARE: Frequent re-cutting of stems keeps a good flow of water up the stem.

Keep away from excess heat and direct sunlight. Remove the lower flowers as they wilt.
TRADE CARE: Best kept at 36-41°F (2-5°C). At these temperatures they can be held for up to 3 days without water; below 36°F (2°C) may stop flower development.

ERIGERON
Fleabane

FAMILY: Compositae
BOTANICAL NAME: *Erigeron speciosus* hybrids
DESCRIPTION: Daisy-like flowers, 2 in (5 cm) across, consist of florets of narrow rays surrounding a centre that is usually yellow or brown. The colours of the petals range from lilac to purple; less common are shades of pink and red. The flowers appear in sprays at the end of stems that are 20-24 in (50-60 cm) long.
TIME TO BUY: When the flowers are starting to open.
VASE LIFE: Approximately 1 week.
SPECIAL HOME CARE: Re-cut the stems frequently, and keep erigeron away from draughts and excess heat to help maintain a high level of humidity. Otherwise, the petals may dry and curl up.
TRADE CARE: Best kept at 36-41°F (2-5°C), although 34-39°F (1-4°C). is also acceptable. Place in water as soon as possible. Storage is not recommended.

ERYNGIUM
Sea Holly

FAMILY: Umbelliferae
BOTANICAL NAME: *Eryngium alpinum, E. giganteum, E. planum*
DESCRIPTION: The flower head consists of a cone up to 1½ in (4 cm) long, surrounded at its base by prominent bracts, both of which are of a metallic blue colour. The stem length is usually between 20-28 in (50-70 cm).
TIME TO BUY: When open. Once cut, it does not continue to develop.
AVAILABILITY: Summer.
VASE LIFE: Approximately 10 days. The foliage tends to turn yellow and dry up well before the flowers.
TRADE CARE: Best kept at 36-41°F (2-5°C). Storage is not recommended.
SUITABLE FOR DRYING

EUCHARIS
Amazon lily

Eucharis grandiflora 'Amazonica'

FAMILY: Amaryliaceae
BOTANICAL NAME: *Eucharis grandiflora* and *E. amazonica*
DESCRIPTION: Daffodil-like, fragrant white flowers, measuring 2 in (5 cm) in diameter. They are borne in terminal umbels of 3-6 blooms. The stem length is 16-20 in (40-50 cm).
TIME TO BUY: The first blooms are showing colour and have begun to open.
AVAILABILITY: All year.
VASE LIFE: Approximately 10 days, during which time the flowers will continue to open.
TRADE CARE: Best kept at 45-50°F (7-10°C), with a high level of humidity. Lower temperatures can cause discoloration and burning of the petals, and eventually stop flower development. Can be kept for 2-4 days without water; once placed in water they will begin to open.

High humidity is important: the flowers should be sprinkled with water. They are usually shipped in air-tight bags that maintain a high level of moisture around the flower, and prevent crushing.

Care should be taken in handling eucharis since they bruise easily.

34

EUCOMIS
Pineapple lily

Eucomis comosa

FAMILY: Liliaceae
BOTANICAL NAME: *Eucomis comosa*
DESCRIPTION: Fragrant, star-shaped flowers, under 1¼in (3 cm) across, appear in profusion along a spike that ends in a tuft of leafy bracts. The flowers are green with a purple centre. The stem length is over 2 ft (60 cm).
TIME TO BUY: When only the lower third of the florets on the spike have opened.
AVAILABILITY: Mainly spring.
VASE LIFE: From 10-14 days.
SPECIAL HOME CARE: Re-cut the stem ends frequently, to encourage opening of the florets. Remove the white section of the stem that does not take up water well.
TRADE CARE: Best kept at 34-36°F (1-2°C) (although 36-41°F (2-5°C)) will not harm the flowers). Can be held for up to 5 days dry; once placed in water, they will begin to open up.

EUPHORBIA

FAMILY: Euphorbiaceae
BOTANICAL NAME: *Euphorbia fulgens*, also known as scarlet plume, flowering spurge; *Euphorbia marginata*, also known as Kenyan euphorbia
DESCRIPTION: *E. fulgens* consists of ½in (1-1.5 cm) flowers that appear alongside the stem, in recurved, wand-like sprays, 1 ft (30 cm) long, at the end of thin, drooping stems. The flowers are mainly orange or red; less commonly, white, salmon pink or lavender. The stem length varies between 2-3 ft (60-90 cm).
   E. marginata consists of small, white flowers that appear at the end of a leafy stem, 20-28 in (50-70 cm) long. In appearance, it looks like variegated foliage with no flowers.
TIME TO BUY: When the majority of the flowers have opened.
AVAILABILITY: Late autumn and winter.
VASE LIFE: *E. fulgens*: approximately 1 week; *E. marginata*: 7-10 days.
SPECIAL HOME CARE: Sear the end of the stem with a flame, or immerse the end in boiling water for a few seconds, in order to stop the loss of latex. Alternatively, re-cut the end of the stem underwater, and the sap will coagulate on its own.
   E. marginata is relatively trouble-free.
   Loss of leaves is very common in euphorbias, and it does not indicate old or poor flowers. Many florists remove the leaves before making an arrangement, so that the leaves will not drop afterwards.
TRADE CARE: Best kept at 45-55°F (7-13°C). Lower temperatures, as well as excess humidity, can cause the flowers to droop. Storage is not recommended.

FORSYTHIA
Golden bell

FAMILY: Oleaceae
BOTANICAL NAME: *Forsythia × intermedia*
DESCRIPTION: Tubular, 1 in (2.5 cm) yellow flowers appear in small clusters (2-4 flowers) close to and along a leafless, woody stem. The stem length can reach over 3 ft (1 m).
   F. × intermedia 'Spectabilis' and 'Lynwood' are the main varieties for cutting. 'Spectabilis' flowers are a clearer yellow, and have woodier and smaller stems than 'Lynwood', whose flowers are a more golden yellow.
TIME TO BUY: When the flowers are closed, with the smallest sign of colour showing.

AVAILABILITY: Winter to early spring.

VASE LIFE: 2 weeks.

SPECIAL HOME CARE: The stems are woody, so cut with secateurs — do not crush them. Immersing the stem ends in hot water will soften the woody tissue, and ease the flow of water up the stem.

There are specific foods for forcing shrubs — if possible, these should be used.

TRADE CARE: In dormant stage, forsythia should be kept at 32-34°F (0-1°C) in a moist, dark atmosphere, for up to one week. Once flowering (or to promote flowering), forsythia should be placed in water with forcing shrub food, at a temperature of 39-41°F (4-5°C).

Forcing shrubs, such as forsythia, need a cold period in their dormant stage before the buds begin to open. In general, forcing shrubs bought before January need a longer period of cold storage than those bought after this date.

FREESIA

FAMILY: Iridiaceae

BOTANICAL NAME: *Freesia* hybrid

DESCRIPTION: Thin stems bear one-sided spikes of 5-8 flowers. The flowers are funnel-shaped, very fragrant and are ¾-1 in (2.5-5 cm) long. They come in single or double forms. The stem length varies from 1-2 ft (30-60 cm). A good freesia should have up to 12 buds, with at least four viable buds (i.e. buds that will open). The main colours are yellow, pink, purple-blue, white, red and orange, in both single and double forms.

TIME TO BUY: When one bud on the spike has opened or is about to burst. In summer, the high temperatures will ensure opening of the buds, but in the winter months care should be taken not to buy them too tight as they may not open properly. Many florists remove the top flower as this tends to wilt well before the rest of the buds.

AVAILABILITY: All year, but mainly winter to spring.

VASE LIFE: Up to 1 week.

SPECIAL HOME CARE: Keep away from draughts, excess heat, and fruit, vegetables and any wilting flowers.

TRADE CARE: Best kept at 36-41°F (2-5°C). In these conditions they can be held for up to 3 days in water. They should always be in water, even when being transported, as they are very susceptible to drying up. Freesias are susceptible to ethylene gas damage.

Prolonged refrigeration will diminish their fragrance.

SUITABLE FOR DRYING

FRITILLARIA
Crown imperial lily

Fritillaria imperialis

FAMILY: Liliaceae

BOTANICAL NAME: *Fritillaria imperialis*

DESCRIPTION: Nodding, tulip-shaped flowers, about 2 in (5 cm) long, are carried in groups of about five at the tops of the stem. Crowning this cluster is a tuft of green leaves. The thick stem is 24-28 in (60-70 cm) in length. The flowers range from yellow to deep red.

TIME TO BUY: When the flowers are starting to open up and are clearly showing colour.

AVAILABILITY: Summer.

VASE LIFE: 1 week to 10 days.

SPECIAL HOME CARE: When re-cutting the stem ends, remove the lower, white section. Change the water frequently, as the stems are easily clogged up with bacteria, and this can stop the flow of water up to the flower.

TRADE CARE: Best kept at 36-41°F (2-5°C). Under these conditions they can be held dry for up to 3 days.

GAILLARDIA
Blanket flower

Gaillardia aristata

FAMILY: Compositae
BOTANICAL NAME: *Gaillardia aristata* hybrids
DESCRIPTION: Daisy-like flowers, 2¾-4 in (7-10 cm) wide, with yellow or red petals surrounding a darker centre. The stem length is around 20-28 in (50-70 cm).
TIME TO BUY: When the flowers have already opened.
AVAILABILITY: Summer.
VASE LIFE: 7-10 days.
TRADE CARE: Best kept at 36-41°F (2-5°C). Storage is not recommended.

GALANTHUS
Snowdrop

Galanthus nivalis

FAMILY: Amaryllidaceae
BOTANICAL NAME: *Galanthus nivalis*
DESCRIPTION: The drooping, white flowers, about 1¼ in (3 cm) long, have three long outer and three short inner petals and appear at the end of short, 8 in (20 cm) stems.
TIME TO BUY: When in bud, but clearly showing colour.
AVAILABILITY: Mainly winter.
VASE LIFE: Approximately 5-7 days.
TRADE CARE: Best kept at 37-41°F (3-5°C).
  Handle galanthus with care, as they bruise easily.

GALTONIA
Summer hyacinth

FAMILY: Liliaceae
BOTANICAL NAME: *Galtonia candicans*
DESCRIPTION: Erect spikes carry 12 or more bell-shaped flowers loosely spaced out on the stem. The flowers are white, with green marks on the petals. The stems reach over 2 ft (60 cm) in length.

TIME TO BUY: When only the lower florets have started to open.

AVAILABILITY: Summer.

VASE LIFE: 10 days.

TRADE CARE: Best kept at 36-41°F (2-5°C). At this temperature can be held for up to 3 days, after which should be placed in water.

GARDENIA
Cape jasmine

Gardenia jasminoides

FAMILY: Rubiaceae

BOTANICAL NAME: *Gardenia jasminoides*

DESCRIPTION: White, waxen, double flowers, 2¾in (7cm) across, are borne at the end of the branches from the leaf axils. The stem length is usually no more than 16in (40cm). They are fragrant.

TIME TO BUY: When the outer petals have opened but are not yet too separated from the stem, and whilst the inner central petals are still closed. Since these flowers have a short vase life, the time of purchase is critical.

AVAILABILITY: Summer.

VASE LIFE: Gardenias have a short vase life of no more than 2-3 days once open.

SPECIAL HOME CARE: Place the flowers in a cool spot, and mist them frequently.

TRADE CARE: Best kept at 32-36°F (0-2°C). At this temperature they can last up to 2 weeks without water, as long as humidity is kept high and/or the flowers are frequently sprinkled with water. Once placed in water, they will immediately open.

Gardenias bruise easily, so handle them as little as possible.

GENISTA
Broom

FAMILY: Leguminoceae

BOTANICAL NAME: *Cytisus canariensis*

DESCRIPTION: Small, ½in (1.5cm) sweet-pea-shaped flowers appear in profusion on leafless branches. The branches, when cut, are usually 16-20in (40-50cm) long. The flowers, naturally whitish-yellow, are often dyed in a variety of colours. The flowers are fragrant.

AVAILABILITY: Spring.

TIME TO BUY: When the majority of the flowers on the branch have begun to open.

VASE LIFE: 7-10 days.

SPECIAL HOME CARE: Keep away from excess heat, fruit, vegetables and wilting flowers, as these may cause flower drop.

TRADE CARE: Best kept at 34-36°F (1-2°C) (although up to 41°F (5°C) will do. If kept at the lower temperature, they can be held for up to 5 days without water. Genista is susceptible to ethylene gas damage.

Genista is usually sold by weight, in bunches of ½-1lb (250-500g). It is graded both by length of stem and by quality. The terminal branches are graded as first-grade genista; the second grade consists of the woodier part of the stem.

GERBERA
Transvaal daisy

FAMILY: Compositae
BOTANICAL NAME: *Gerbera* hybrids
DESCRIPTION: Daisy-like flowers, 2-5 in (5-12 cm) across, at the end of a single, leafless thin stem. The stem length varies between 10-24 in (25-60 cm). The flowers, that come in single and double forms, have a yellow or a dark centre. The large range of colours includes yellow, orange, cream, white, pink, red and purple.

The most common varieties are hybrids from *Gerbera jamesonii* and *G. viridifolia*.
TIME TO BUY: When the outer petals are fully expanded but before the florets that make up the disc centre are mature (i.e. before pollen is shed). If in doubt buy over- rather than under-developed, as gerbera that is harvested too soon will wilt.
AVAILABILITY: All year round, but mainly spring.
VASE LIFE: 1 week.
SPECIAL HOME CARE: If the stems are limp, place them in a tall container, with the stems hanging into the water, and the heads supported by chicken wire. This way they will drink water, and become straight and sturdy. If gerbera stems are sturdy but need straightening, keep them out of water for approximately 12 hours or until they are limp, and then treat as given above. Cut off the heel of the stem, if it has not already been removed as it does not take in water well.

Gerbera stems are easily blocked, so re-cut the stem ends frequently, and change the water regularly, adding a drop of bleach each time. Gerberas are best placed in a cool spot, away from excess heat and direct sunlight.
TRADE CARE: Best kept at 36-41°F (2-5°C). Place in water as soon as possible. Special care should be taken in handling them as they bruise easily.

Gerbera should be placed whenever possible in a cold room before use, to remove excess heat and ensure a longer-lasting life. If using bleach, do not use more than 0.5 ml of 10 per cent chlorine solution to 1.7 pints (1 litre) of water.

Gerberas are usually packed in trays, each flower individually secured in the box. Sometimes they are packed loose, with a clear plastic cup protecting each flower head. A new method, that is becoming increasingly popular, is to insert the gerbera stem in a clear plastic tube that is then sealed to the stem with heat, making the flower stand up straight.

GINGER LILY
Red ginger, Ostrich plume, Torch ginger

Alpinia purpurata (Ginger lily)

FAMILY: Zingiberaeceae
BOTANICAL NAME: *Alpinia purpurata*
DESCRIPTION: The flower head, 8-10 in (20-25 cm) long, is made up of thick, shiny red bracts at the end of a strong stem that measures up to 3 ft (1 m).
TIME TO BUY: The flowers should be open.
AVAILABILITY: All year round.
VASE LIFE: Up to 3 weeks.
TRADE CARE: Best kept at 47-55°F (8-13°C). Without water, they can be kept for over one week. The use of flower food will help keep the water clean, but otherwise has not been shown to prolong the vase life of the flower.

GLADIOLUS
Sword lily

FAMILY: Iridaceae
BOTANICAL NAME: *Gladiolus* hybrids
DESCRIPTION: Gladiolus flowers are arranged on a thick flower stem, forming a spike. The florets, arranged tightly or loosely, always face one way. The shape of the flower differs from one type to another,

and most colours, except for true blue, are available. The flowers vary in size from 2¾-5 in (7-12 cm), on spikes 18-30 in (45-75 cm) long, on stems that can reach up to 4 ft (120 cm) in length.

LARGE-FLOWERED VARIETIES are hybrids, with 10-16 large flowers, on a spike that measures 20 in (50 cm). The stem length is 2½-4 ft (80-120 cm) long.

MEDIUM-SIZED VARIETIES are mainly *Primulinus* hybrids, with smaller flowers, loosely arranged on a 16 in (40 cm) long spike. The stem length is 2-2½ft (60-80 cm).

SMALL AND MINIATURE GLADIOLI have smaller flowers, usually loosely arranged on 10-14 in (25-35 cm) long spikes. The stem length is under 2 ft (60 cm). This group includes varieties of G. × *colvillei* and the Butterfly hybrids.

TIME TO BUY: In tight bud stage, with 2-3 leaves remaining on the stem, and from 1-5 buds showing colour.

AVAILABILITY: All year round but mainly summer, except for the smaller types that are almost only available in the summer months.

VASE LIFE: 10 days to 2 weeks. The larger varieties have a longer vase life than the smaller varieties.

TRADE CARE: Best kept at 36-41°F (2-5°C). Lower temperature can cause frost damage to the flowers. Storage without water is not recommended.

At low temperatures and in water, gladioli can be kept in the bud stage for 7 days, and in the opening stage, for one more week. If keeping flowers for any amount of time in a cold room, keep the light on — this makes sure the buds open and the colour is not dulled.

To reduce stem curvature and force the upper flowers to open up, pinch off the 2-3 top buds before storage.

The flowers should always be shipped and kept in an upright position so as to avoid stem curvature. The use of food solutions will promote bud opening.

GLORIOSA
Glory lily

FAMILY: Liliaceae
BOTANICAL NAME: *Gloriosa rothschildiana*, G. *superba*
DESCRIPTION: 2¾-4 in (7-10 cm) flowers that have six narrow, reflexed petals that are crisped and curled at the margins. The flowers are red and yellow. They are sold either on short, 8 in (20 cm) stems, with no leaves, or on long, up to 2 ft (60 cm) stems, with 3-5 smaller flower heads on each stem. G. *rothschildiana*

has red petals with yellow, waxy edges; G. *superba* has yellow petals that turn orange to red at the tips, that are more crisped.

TIME TO BUY: When fully open.
AVAILABILITY: All year round.
VASE LIFE: 5-10 days.
SPECIAL HOME CARE: Spray the flowers frequently with water to maintain a high moisture level. Keep away from draughts, direct sunlight and excess heat. If the flowers are limp, immerse them entirely in water for a few minutes.
TRADE CARE: Best kept at 34-36°F (1-2°C) (although up to 41°F (5°C) will do). It is important to maintain a high level of humidity. The flowers come packed in airtight bags, that not only help maintain the high level of moisture, but protect the delicate petals. They are best kept in these airtight bags until used.

GODETIA
Satin flower

Godetia grandiflora

Godetias are sometimes included under Clarkias.
FAMILY: Onagraceae
BOTANICAL NAME: *Godetia grandiflora*
DESCRIPTION: Clusters of funnel-shaped flowers, which are 2 in (5 cm) across. There are single and double forms, in shades of orange, red and violet/

pink. The stem length is 12-20 in (30-50 cm).

TIME TO BUY: When the flowers have already opened.

AVAILABILITY: Spring to summer.

VASE LIFE: Approximately 1 week.

TRADE CARE: Best kept at 36-41°F (2-5°C). Storage is not recommended.

GOMPHRENA
Globe amaranth

FAMILY: Amaranthaceae

BOTANICAL NAME: *Gomphrena globosa*

DESCRIPTION: The round flower head, ³/₄-1¹/₂ in (2-4 cm) across, appears at the end of a 12-20 in (30-50 cm) long stem. The flower head is made up of tiny, clover-like, fluffy flowers that come in white, orange, pink and purple.

TIME TO BUY: Just before the blooms on the flower head are fully open.

AVAILABILITY: Summer.

VASE LIFE: Approximately 1 week.

TRADE CARE: Best kept at 36-41°F (2-5°C). Storage is not recommended.

SUITABLE FOR DRYING

GREVILLEA

Grevillea banksia 'Red Robin'

FAMILY: Proteaceae

BOTANICAL NAME: *Grevillea* species

DESCRIPTION: Small, cone-shaped, red flowers on stems 20-32 in (50-80 cm) long that are covered with pine-like foliage.

TIME TO BUY: When fully open.

AVAILABILITY: All year round.

VASE LIFE: Up to 2 weeks.

SPECIAL HOME CARE: The woody stems should be cut with secateurs, not crushed.

TRADE CARE: Best kept at 36-41°F (2-5°C). At these temperatures they can be held for up to 5 days without water.

SUITABLE FOR DRYING

GYPSOPHILA
Baby's breath

FAMILY: Caryophyllaceae

BOTANICAL NAME: *Gypsophila* species

DESCRIPTION: Loose panicles of tiny flowers are produced in quantity on branched stems, giving an airy effect. The flowers are usually white, but some pink varieties are also available. The stems, once cut, vary in length between 12-28 in (30-70 cm).

The main varieties include G. *paniculata*, of which smaller-flowering varieties include 'Bristol Fairy' (white), 'Flamingo' (pink); larger-flowering are those of 'Giant Bristol Fairy' (white), 'Perfecta' and 'Bristol Fairy Perfecta' (white); G. *elegans*, such as 'Roem Van Rijnsburg' (white) and 'Rosea' (pink).

TIME TO BUY: When two-thirds of the flowers on the branch are fully open. It is not advisable to buy gypsophila if no florets are in full bloom — no flowers may open up at all.

AVAILABILITY: All year round, but mainly summer.

VASE LIFE: Although delicate-looking, gypsophila is a hardy flower that will last 2 days in the opening stage, and 7-10 days in an open stage.

SPECIAL HOME CARE: Keep away from fruit, vegetables or damaged flowers, and from heat and draughts.

TRADE CARE: Best kept at 36-39°F (2-4°C). Do not keep without water for more than 2 days. In water, and in cooled conditions, they can be held for up to 4-5 days. Good air circulation will prevent botrytis damage, and a high level of humidity will promote good flower development.

Opening solutions with 5-10 per cent sucrose have proved effective; silver treatment has shown results in extending flower life. Gypsophila is very sensitive to ethylene gas damage.

SUITABLE FOR DRYING

HAEMANTHUS
Blood lily

Haemanthus katharinae

HAMAMELIS
Witch hazel, Chinese witch hazel

Hamamelis mollis

FAMILY: Amaryllidaceae
BOTANICAL NAME: *Haemanthus katherinae*
DESCRIPTION: The 6 in (15 cm) wide spherical flower head is composed of tiny red, salmon or orange flowers, giving a shaving brush appearance. The stem length is usually no more than 12-16 in (30-40 cm).
TIME TO BUY: When the flower head is starting to open.
AVAILABILITY: Mainly summer.
VASE LIFE: 1 week.
TRADE CARE: Best kept at 45-50°F (7-10°C). Lower temperatures can cause discoloration of petals and interrupt flower development. Place in water as soon as possible.

FAMILY: Hamamelidaceae
BOTANICAL NAME: *Hamamelis mollis*
DESCRIPTION: The ¾-1½ in (2-4 cm) wide flowers are fragrant and have a spidery appearance, with yellow flat petals that are flushed red at the base. They are thickly clustered along the leafless twigs that are usually 16-20 in (40-50 cm) long.
TIME TO BUY: When the flowers are starting to open.
AVAILABILITY: Winter.
VASE LIFE: 7-9 days.
SPECIAL HOME CARE: The woody stems can be softened by placing them in boiling water for a few seconds, which will also ease the flow of water up the stem. Do not crush the stems, cut them using secateurs.
TRADE CARE: Best kept at 36-41°F (2-5°C). Place in water as soon as possible, as the petals dry up quickly. Storage is not recommended.

HEATHER
Erica, Heath, Calluna

Erica carnea 'Myretown Ruby'

Strictly speaking, heath is only applicable to *Erica*, and heather, only to *Calluna*. In practice, and in the comments that follow, the terms are used loosely for both genera and others such as *Daboecia*.
FAMILY: Ericaceae
BOTANICAL NAME: *Erica*, *Calluna* and *Daboecia* species
DESCRIPTION: The small, bell-shaped flowers are single, sometimes double, and come in shades of pink, purple, red or white, and occasionally bi-coloured. They appear in loose terminal racemes, on stems usually no more than 8-12 in (20-30 cm) in length.
WHEN TO BUY: When the flowers are open.
AVAILABILITY: Mainly winter and spring.
VASE LIFE: Approximately 1 week.
SPECIAL HOME CARE: Frequent re-cutting and additional misting of the flowers will maintain a high moisture level, and stop the shedding of flowers.
TRADE CARE: Best kept at 36-41°F (2-5°C). At these temperatures they can be held for up to 5 days in water. Dry storage is not recommended.
SUITABLE FOR DRYING

HEBE

Hebes were formerly included under *Veronica*.
FAMILY: Scrophulariaceae
BOTANICAL NAME: *Hebe × andersonii* and *H. speciosa* hybrids
DESCRIPTION: Small flowers, white or violet, are borne in terminal racemes or short, 2-4 in (5-10 cm) long spikes. The flowers are formed by four unequal-sized petals that are pointed or rounded.
TIME TO BUY: When the majority of the flowers on the cluster or spike have opened.
AVAILABILITY: Summer.
VASE LIFE: Approximately 1 week.
SPECIAL HOME CARE: As the flowers on the cluster open up, the lower florets tend to dry off and should be removed. Keep hebe away from excess heat, wilting flowers, fruit, vegetables and household gases.
TRADE CARE: Best kept at 36-41°F (2-5°C). Place in water as soon as possible. Storage is not recommended. Hebe is sensitive to ethylene gas damage.

HELENIUM

Helenium autumnale

FAMILY: Compositae
BOTANICAL NAME: *Helenium autumnale*
DESCRIPTION: Daisy-like flowers, 1½-2 in (4-5 cm) across, with a central dark disc, surrounded by petals in yellow or shades of red. They appear at the end of branchlets, off a single stem. The stem length is approximately 2 ft (60 cm).
TIME TO BUY: When the majority of the flowers on the spray have opened.
AVAILABILITY: Summer.
VASE LIFE: 8-10 days.
TRADE CARE: Best kept at 36-41°F (2-5°C). Storage is not recommended.

HELIANTHUS
Sunflower

Helianthus

FAMILY: Compositae
BOTANICAL NAME: *Helianthus annuus, H. decapetalus*
DESCRIPTION: Annual or perennial, daisy-like flowers, from 2-10 in (5-25 cm) across, with yellow petals surrounding a large brown or yellow disc. They stand singly or in sprays at the end of stems that vary between 20-39 in (50-100 cm). The flowers usually have single forms, but occasionally are double.
 The most popular are the large varieties such as

H. decapetalus 'Soleil d'Or' (semi-double) and single and double forms of *H. annuus*.
TIME TO BUY: When the flower is open.
AVAILABILITY: Spray sunflowers are available mainly in the summer, whilst single, traditional sunflowers are available in late summer and early autumn.
VASE LIFE: 7-10 days.
TRADE CARE: Best kept at 36-41°F (2-5°C). Storage is not recommended.

HELICHRYSUM
Everlasting flower, Straw flower

FAMILY: Compositae
BOTANICAL NAME: *Helichrysum bracteatum*
DESCRIPTION: Double, 2 in (5 cm) flowers with crisp, papery petals in a wide variety of colours, including red, orange, pink, yellow and white. The stems are 12-20 in (30-50 cm) long.
TIME TO BUY: Before they are fully open, but are showing the central disc.
AVAILABILITY: Summer.
VASE LIFE: 7-10 days.
TRADE CARE: Best kept at 36-41°F (2-5°C). Place in water as soon as possible. Storage is not recommended.
SUITABLE FOR DRYING

HELICONIA
Lobster claw

FAMILY: Musaceae
BOTANICAL NAME: *Heliconia* species
DESCRIPTION: Brightly-coloured, erect or drooping flowers consisting of stiff, shiny bracts that are boat-shaped and tightly packed together. The flower head can vary from 5-16 in (12-40 cm) long, and the stem length is usually over 20 in (50 cm), up to 3 ft (100 cm). The flowers are red, orange, yellow and are sometimes tinted with green.
 Heliconias can be roughly divided into erect and drooping flowers. There are many species, of which the most popular are: *H. humilis* or lobster claw (red), pink and green heliconia (*H. elongata*), *H. ivorea* (yellow), *H. andromeda* (reddish orange) and *H. caraibea* (red) — all these are erect. The main hanging variety is *H. pendula* (orange-red).
TIME TO BUY: When fully developed. Once the flower has been cut, further opening of the bracts does not occur.
AVAILABILITY: All year round.

VASE LIFE: From 10 days to 2 weeks. No special care is required.
TRADE CARE: Best kept at around 45-47°F (7-8°C). Lower temperatures can cause damage to the bracts. Place in water as soon as possible, to prevent drying up of the bracts. Preservative solutions have shown no effect on prolonging the life of heliconias.

HELIPTERUM
Rhodanthe and Acrolinum

Helipterum roseum

FAMILY: Compositae
BOTANICAL NAME: *Helipterum manglesii*
DESCRIPTION: Daisy-like, straw-textured flowers, usually double, 1 in (2.5 cm) across that appear singly at the end of thin stems, 1-2 ft (30-60 cm) long. The main colours are shades of pink or white, with a yellow centre.
TIME TO BUY: When the flowers are open.
AVAILABILITY: Summer.
VASE LIFE: Approximately 1 week.
TRADE CARE: Best kept at 36-41°F (2-5°C). Place in water as soon as possible. Storage is not recommended.
SUITABLE FOR DRYING

HELLEBORUS
Christmas rose, Lenten rose

Helleborus niger

FAMILY: Ranunculaceae
BOTANICAL NAME: *H. niger* (also known as Christmas Rose); *H. orientalis* (also known as Lenten Rose)
DESCRIPTION: Saucer-shaped flowers, 1½-2 in (4-5 cm) across, are formed by a single row of five broad, overlapping petals, surrounding a small central cluster of long, golden-coloured anthers. *H. niger* has white, saucer-shaped petals; *H. orientalis* has white, pink or purple (sometimes with spots), cup-shaped petals.
TIME TO BUY: When already open but before the petals are completely separated from the centre.
AVAILABILITY: Winter.
VASE LIFE: 5-7 days.
TRADE CARE: Best kept at 36-41°F (2-5°C). Place in water as soon as possible. Storage is not recommended.
SUITABLE FOR DRYING

HESPERIS
Damask violet, Sweet rocket

Hesperis matronalis

FAMILY: Cruciferae
BOTANICAL NAME: *Hesperis matronalis*
DESCRIPTION: 18 in (45 cm) long spikes with small, cross-shaped lilac or white flowers that have oblong petals. When cut, the stem length is 24-32 in (60-80 cm).
AVAILABILITY: Summer.
TIME TO BUY: When the flowers have started to open.
VASE LIFE: Approximately 1 week.
TRADE CARE: Best kept at 47-55°F (8-13°C). Lower temperatures may cause damage to the flowers. Place in water as soon as possible. Storage is not recommended.

HEUCHERA
Coral flower

Heuchera sanguinea

FAMILY: Saxifragaceae
BOTANICAL NAME: *Heuchera sanguinea* hybrids
DESCRIPTION: Slender stems, 16-20 in (40-50 cm) long, carry panicles of tiny, bright bell-shaped flowers usually red, but also available in pink, white and yellow. The panicles are 8-12 in (20-30 cm) long. Most are hybrids of *H. sanguinea*.
TIME TO BUY: When at least half the flowers on the panicle have opened.
AVAILABILITY: Summer.
VASE LIFE: Approximately 1 week.
TRADE CARE: Best kept at 45-55°F (7-13°C). Place in water as soon as possible. Storage is not recommended.
SUITABLE FOR DRYING

HIBISCUS

Hibiscus rosa-sinensis

HOSTA
Funkia, Plantain lily

Hosta fortunei 'Albopicta'

FAMILY: Malvaceae
BOTANICAL NAME: *Hibiscus rosa-sinensis*
DESCRIPTION: The flowers, 4-5 in (10-12 cm) across, are widely funnel-shaped, mostly single, although double forms can also be found. They appear close to the leaf joints on slender short branchlets. The stem, when cut, is 20-24 in (50-60 cm) long. The main colours are red, yellow, pink and salmon.
TIME TO BUY: When the flowers are starting to open.
AVAILABILITY: All year round, but mainly autumn.
VASE LIFE: Hibiscus have a short vase life of 3-5 days.
SPECIAL HOME CARE: Mist the flowers frequently to maintain a high level of humidity.
TRADE CARE: Hibiscus are not very common as cut flowers due to their short vase life. Best kept at 45-55°F (7-13°C). Place in water as soon as possible. Storage is not recommended.

FAMILY: Liliaceae
BOTANICAL NAME: *Hosta* species
DESCRIPTION: Funnel-shaped, 2 in (5 cm) flowers appear on spikes at the end of a straight, almost leafless stem. The flowers are white or lilac. The spike can reach 12 in (30 cm), and the total stem, when cut, 16-24 in (40-60 cm).
TIME TO BUY: When the majority of the flowers on the spike are in bud and showing colour. Only a few should be open at time of purchase.
AVAILABILITY: Summer.
VASE LIFE: 3-4 days in the opening stage, and a further 4-5 days opening.
SPECIAL HOME CARE: Handle the flowers with care as they bruise easily.
TRADE CARE: Best kept at 36-41°F (2-5°C). At this temperature they can be held for up to 3 days without water, or one week in water.

HYACINTH
Common hyacinth, Dutch hyacinth

For Summer hyacinth, see Galtonia
For Grape hyacinth, see Muscari.
FAMILY: Liliaceae
BOTANICAL NAME: *Hyacinthus orientalis*
DESCRIPTION: Compact spikes, 4-6in (10-15cm) long, of bell-shaped flowers that are mainly white or blue, although purple, pink, red and yellow varieties are also found. The stem length, when cut, is no more than 8-12in (20-30cm). The flowers are fragrant.

Hybrids from *H. orientalis*, usually known as Dutch hyacinths, are used as cut flowers.
TIME TO BUY: When the lower petals have coloured and are starting to open. They are sometimes sold in an earlier stage, and are then called sprig hyacinths.
AVAILABILITY: Mainly winter and early spring.
VASE LIFE: Over 1 week.
TRADE CARE: Best kept at 36-41°F (2-5°C), although for any prolonged period, 41°F (5°C) is recommended as they can suffer from cold damage. Under these conditions they can be held for 2-3 days without water, and up to 5 days in water. Prolonged refrigeration will reduce fragrance.

HYDRANGEA

FAMILY: Hydrangeaceae
BOTANICAL NAME: *Hydrangea* species
DESCRIPTION: Small, star-shaped flowers are packed closely together, forming a rounded or pyramidal large cluster. The flowers are generally blue, pink or white. The stem, when cut, is usually 16-20in (40-50cm) long.

The main varieties are from *H. macrophylla* (rounded cluster) and *H. paniculata* (pyramidal cluster).
TIME TO BUY: When the majority of the florets are starting to open.
AVAILABILITY: Summer.
VASE LIFE: Approximately 1 week.
SPECIAL HOME CARE: Immerse the stem ends in boiling water or sear with a flame, to stop the bleeding of latex, that causes premature wilting.
TRADE CARE: Best kept at 36-41°F (2-5°C). Place in water as soon as possible. Storage is not recommended.
SUITABLE FOR DRYING

HYPERICUM
St John's wort

Hypericum elatum

FAMILY: Guttiferae
BOTANICAL NAME: *Hypericum elatum*
DESCRIPTION: Cup-shaped flowers, 1in (2.5cm) wide, that open up flat and have yellow petals surrounding a central boss of golden stamens. They appear profusely at the end of short branchlets. The stem, when cut, is approximately 2ft (60cm) long.
TIME TO BUY: When the flowers have opened but have not separated from the central stamens.
AVAILABILITY: Late summer and early autumn.
VASE LIFE: 4-6 days.
TRADE CARE: Best kept at 36-41°F (2-5°C). Place in water as soon as possible. Storage is not recommended.

IBERIS
Candytuft

Iberis umbellata

FAMILY: Cruciferae

BOTANICAL NAME: *Iberis armara* (also known as hyacinth flowered candytuft), *I. umbellata*

DESCRIPTION: Small, cross-shaped flowers are borne in 2 in (5 cm) wide, broad terminal racemes. The main colours are purple, pink and white. The stems, when cut, are a maximum of 16 in (40 cm).

AVAILABILITY: Mainly summer.

TIME TO BUY: When the flowers have started to open.

VASE LIFE: 5-6 days.

TRADE CARE: Best kept at 36-41°F (2-5°C). At these temperatures they can be held in water for up to 3 days.

IRIS

FAMILY: Iridaceae

BOTANICAL NAME: *Iris* hybrids

DESCRIPTION: 4-6 in (10-15 cm) wide flower head that consists of three outer petals, three inner petals and three styles projecting in between. The main colours are purple, yellow and white. The stem, when cut, is 18-24 in (45-60 cm) long.

Most cut flowers are varieties of Dutch irises. The main ones are 'Professor Blaauw' and 'Ideal' (blue), 'White Excelsior' (white) and 'Golden Harvest' (yellow).

TIME TO BUY: When the buds are showing colour but have not yet opened. As a rule, 'Professor Blaauw' should be bought in a more developed stage than other varieties.

In the winter months, it is advisable to buy iris with more colour showing than in the summer months, when there is less danger of the bud not opening. If the tip of the flower, when closed, is dry, the flower will not open properly.

AVAILABILITY: Mostly autumn and winter months.

VASE LIFE: 3-7 days.

SPECIAL HOME CARE: Keep away from excess heat, fruit, vegetables and any wilting flowers. Re-cut the stem ends frequently, and remove the lower white section that does not take up water easily.

TRADE CARE: Best kept cooled at 36-41°F (2-5°C).. Iris can be held dry for 1-2 weeks at 32°F (0°C). In water, at temperatures between 36-41°F (2-5°C), flower opening can be retarded for 5-7 days. In water, at room temperature, iris will open up immediately. Iris stems dry up easily, so frequent re-cutting of stems is advisable. Iris is sensitive to ethylene gas damage.

SUITABLE FOR DRYING

IXIA
African corn lily

FAMILY: Iridaceae

BOTANICAL NAME: *Ixia* hybrid

DESCRIPTION: Star-shaped flowers, 1-1½ in (2.5-4 cm) wide, consist of six petals surrounding a dark centre. They appear in clusters of 4-6 flowers on tall wiry stems. The stems, when cut, are 18 in (45 cm) long. Colours are white, pink, purple, red or orange.

TIME TO BUY: When the flowers show some colour but have not opened. Do not buy ixia that is too immature, as it may not open at all.

AVAILABILITY: Spring and summer months.

VASE LIFE: 7-10 days, during which time the buds will continue to open up.

SPECIAL HOME CARE: Keep ixia away from excess heat, fruit, vegetables and any wilting flowers.

TRADE CARE: Best kept at 32-34°F (0-1°C) dry, for up to 3 days. In water, their flowering can be retarded for 3-4 days at temperatures between 36-41°F (2-5°C). They are sensitive to ethylene gas damage.

IXORA

Ixora hybrid

FAMILY: Rubiaceae
BOTANICAL NAME: *Ixora javanica*
DESCRIPTION: Waxy, tubular flowers with spreading lobes appear in clusters. The main colours are shades of red, orange and pink. They measure 2 in (5 cm) long. The stems, when cut, reach 20-28 in (50-70 cm) in length.
TIME TO BUY: When the first 2-3 florets have opened.
AVAILABILITY: All year round.
VASE LIFE: 5-6 days.
SPECIAL HOME CARE: Frequent re-cutting is advised, as the stem ends tend to be easily obstructed.
TRADE CARE: Best kept at 37-41°F (3-5°C). Lower temperatures may interrupt flower development. If kept dry for any length of time, ixora flowers will droop, and rarely recover.

KANGAROO PAW
Anigozanthos, Kangaroo feet

FAMILY: Haemodoraceae
BOTANICAL NAME: *Anigozanthos* species
DESCRIPTION: Unusual, woolly flowers, 1½-3 in (4-

8 cm) long, with a reflexed lip. The stem, when cut, reaches up to 3 ft (1 m) in height. The most cultivated species is *Anigozanthus flavidus*, with yellow or yellow-brownish-green flowers. *A. manglesii* has larger flowers, yellowy-green with a red border; *A. rufus* is mainly red. The black kangaroo paw (*Macropidia imperia*) comes from a different family, but is similar to and commonly known as kangaroo paw.
TIME TO BUY: When fully developed.
AVAILABILITY: All year round.
VASE LIFE: Approximately 10 days.
SPECIAL HOME CARE: Frequent re-cutting of the stem ends will keep the flowers from drying up.
TRADE CARE: Best kept at approximately 41°F (5°C). At this temperature, they can be held for 4-6 days without water. On unpacking they usually look limp, but revive once placed in water.
SUITABLE FOR DRYING

KNIPHOFIA
Red hot poker, Torch lily, Tritoma

Kniphofia uvaria

FAMILY: Liliaceae
BOTANICAL NAME: *Kniphofia* hybrids
DESCRIPTION: Tight, terminal spikes are densely

packed with tubular flowers with their open ends pointing obliquely downwards. There is one spike per stem, and the stem reaches 24-32 in (60-80 cm) in length. They come in shades of red, orange and yellow. All the main varieties grown are hybrids.

TIME TO BUY: When the lower florets are open, or are clearly showing colour and are starting to open.

AVAILABILITY: Mainly summer.

VASE LIFE: 7-10 days, during which time the florets continue to open up.

TRADE CARE: Best kept at 36-41°F (2-5°C). Under these conditions they can be held in water for 4-5 days.

LAVATERA
Mallow

Lavatera trimestris

FAMILY: Malvaceae

BOTANICAL NAME: *Lavatera trimestris*

DESCRIPTION: Trumpet-shaped, 4 in (10 cm) wide flowers are produced on the axils of the upper leaves of the branchlets. The overall stem length is usually 20-24 in (50-60 cm). The main colour is pink, although white varieties are also available.

The main varieties are 'Mont Blanc' (white) and 'Loveliness', 'Tanagra', 'Silver Cup' and 'Mont Rose' (pink).

TIME TO BUY: When the flowers have begun to open but are not yet lying flat..

AVAILABILITY: Summer.

VASE LIFE: Approximately 1 week.

TRADE CARE: Best kept at 36-41°F (2-5°C). Storage is not recommended.

LAVENDER
Lavandula

Lavandula spica

FAMILY: Labiatae

BOTANICAL NAME: *Lavandula spica*

DESCRIPTION: Small, grey/blue flowers on 2-2½ in (5-6 cm) long spikes appear at the end of 16-20 in (40-50 cm) long stems. Some white varieties also exist but are less common. They are not very showy flowers, and are mainly sought for their fragrance.

Although lavender is a long-lasting flower, it is used more as a dried flower than as a fresh flower.

TIME TO BUY: When the majority of the flowers on the spike have opened.

AVAILABILITY: Summer.

VASE LIFE: Fresh lavender has a vase life of over 10 days.

TRADE CARE: Best kept cooled, between 36-41°F (2-5°C). At these temperatures they can be held up to 3

days dry, and one week in water. Prolonged cooling will diminish the flowers' fragrance.
SUITABLE FOR DRYING: When dried, lavender keeps its fragrance.

LEONOTIS
Lion's ear

Leonotis leonorus

FAMILY: Labiatae
BOTANICAL NAME: *Leonotis leonorus*
DESCRIPTION: The two-lipped, orange flowers are small, and appear in densely showy whorls at the end of a stem that, when cut, reaches 24-32 in (60-80 cm) in length.
TIME TO BUY: When fully open.
AVAILABILITY: Mainly winter.
VASE LIFE: 1 week to 10 days.
TRADE CARE: Best kept at 36-41°F (2-5°C).

LEONTOPODIUM
Edelweiss

Leontopodium alpinum

FAMILY: Compositae
BOTANICAL NAME: *Leontopodium alpinum*
DESCRIPTION: Small, groundsel-like flowers, 2 in (5 cm) across, are surrounded by woolly bracts. They stand at the end of a short stem that, when cut, is usually no more than 8-12 in (20-30 cm) long.
TIME TO BUY: When the flowers are starting to open.
AVAILABILITY: Summer.
VASE LIFE: 6-8 days.
TRADE CARE: Best kept at 36-41°F (2-5°C). Storage is not recommended.
SUITABLE FOR DRYING

LEUCADENDRON

Leucadendron saliginum

FAMILY: Proteaceae

BOTANICAL NAME: *Leucadendron* species

DESCRIPTION: Erect bushy branches, dense with leaves, that increase in size towards the flower head, and generally turn orange or red at the tips. The terminal leaves almost conceal the flower head, that consists of stiff, usually colourful bracts surrounding a cone (in the female forms), and a small, inconspicuous flower (in the male forms). The stem length varies from 12-32 in (30-80 cm) depending on the variety.

L. salignum has reddish-orange bracts: 'Safari Sunset' and 'Safari Glow' (up to 32 in (80 cm) long), 'Red Gem' (up to 24 in (60 cm) long), 'Fire Glow' (up to 20 in (50 cm) long.)

L. argenteum, or silver tree, has silver-green leaves, up to 28 in (70 cm) long.

Other, less common types, consist of leaves surrounding a terminal small cone. They are shrub-like with stems, when cut, usually 18 in (45 cm) in length. *L. discolor* (male form) has showy yellow bracts with red edges, surrounding a red, cone-like flower; *L. platyspermum* (male form) has yellow leaves surrounding a small, fluffy flower head.

There are numerous other types, but the above are the main ones sold commercially.

TIME TO BUY: When the flower head has developed. Once cut, they rarely continue to develop.

AVAILABILITY: Summer.

VASE LIFE: 2-3 weeks. No special care is required.

TRADE CARE: Leucadendrons keep well at room temperature, but are best kept cooled, at between 36-41°F (2-5°C) if they are to be held for any length of time. They can be kept dry for up to 7 days in controlled temperature conditions.

Usually, the leaves, which are stiff, are 'reflexed' or curved down in order to expose the concealed flower head. If not done at source, the leaves can be reflexed on arrival.

SUITABLE FOR DRYING

LEUCOSPERMUM
Pincushion protea

Leucospermum cordifolium

FAMILY: Proteaceae
BOTANICAL NAME: *Leucospermum* species
DESCRIPTION: The flower heads, about 5 in (12 cm) across, consist of colourful styles forming a dome shape, and stand, usually singly, at the end of a woody stem. The flower heads are orangy-red. The stem length varies between 16-24 in (40-60 cm). The main species include *L. pattersonni*, *L. cordifolium*, *L. cuneiforme*, *L. reflexum*, *L. lineare* and *L. truncatum*.
TIME TO BUY: When fully developed.
AVAILABILITY: Mainly autumn and winter.
VASE LIFE: Up to 10 days.
SPECIAL HOME CARE: The stems are woody, and should be cut with secateurs, but not crushed. The stems can be softened by immersion in boiling water for a few seconds, to ease the flow of water up to the flower.
TRADE CARE: Best kept at cooled temperatures between 36-41°F (2-5°C). At controlled temperatures, they can be held for up to 4 days dry, or one week in water. Provide good air circulation as they are prone to rotting.

They are the most delicate and short-lived of the proteas, and should be packed with care for re-shipping as they are easily crushed.

LIATRIS
Gayfeather, Button snakeroot, Kansas godfather

FAMILY: Compositae
BOTANICAL NAME: *Liatris spicata*
DESCRIPTION: Very small flowers appear in dense spikes, 6 in (15 cm) or more long. The stem length varies between 24-32 in (60-80 cm). Mauve, pink or white flowers.
TIME TO BUY: Liatris opens from the top downwards. Buy when only the top blooms have opened.
AVAILABILITY: All year round.
VASE LIFE: 10-14 days.
SPECIAL HOME CARE: Change the water frequently, as liatris pollutes the water at a rapid rate, which obstructs the flow of water up to the flower head. The flowers do not usually open up all the way down the spike.
TRADE CARE: Best kept at 36-41°F (2-5°C), preferably 36-37°F (2-3°C). In these conditions they can be kept for up to 5 days without water, or one week in water. If storing, maintain good air circulation and low temperatures, as they are susceptible to botrytis.
SUITABLE FOR DRYING

LILAC
Syringa

FAMILY: Oleaceae
BOTANICAL NAME: *Syringa vulgaris*
DESCRIPTION: Erect pyramidal panicles, 6-10 in (15-25 cm) long, are formed by small, star-shaped flowers that are single or double. The stem, when cut, is over 2 ft (60 cm) in length. Popular varieties include 'Madame Florent Stepman' (white), 'Lavaliensis' (pink), 'Andenken an Ludwig Spaeth' (mauve) and 'Hugo Koster' (purplish-red).
TIME TO BUY: When the flowers have started to open.
AVAILABILITY: Winter and spring.
VASE LIFE: 5-7 days.
SPECIAL HOME CARE: Do not mix lilac with other flowers (except for holly and forcing shrubs) as its sap can reduce the vase life of the other flowers — unless the lilac has been left to stand on its own in water for 24 hours, and then, without re-cutting the stem end, it can be included with other flowers.

Check the water level of the container frequently, as lilac takes up a lot of water. The addition of flower food can extend the vase life of lilac up to 10 days.

When re-cutting the stems of lilac, use secateurs rather than crushing them. Immersion of the woody stems in boiling water for a few seconds will not only soften the woody tissue for cutting, but will also ease the flow of water up to the flowers.
TRADE CARE: Best kept at 36-39°F (2-4°C). It can be kept for as long as 3-7 days in these conditions, in a dark, moist atmosphere. Lilac is best shipped and kept in water.

LILY

FAMILY: Liliaceae
BOTANICAL NAME: *Lilium* species
DESCRIPTION: The flowers are 4-5 in (10-13 cm) across, and can be cup-shaped with recurved tips, cup-shaped opening flat or trumpet-shaped. They appear on short branchlets, at the end of the stem, and can be upright, pendant or outward-facing. The stem, when cut, varies between 20-35 in (50-90 cm), and on average there are 3-6 flowers per stem. The flowers are often specked or freckled. The main colours are orange, yellow, white, pink and dark red.

The cut flower varieties, generally produced from hybrids, can be divided according to their shape and size:
MID CENTURY LILIES (also known as Asian hybrids):

Cup-shaped with recurved tips, 4-5 in (10-13 cm) across, with 3 and up to 12 flowers per stem. The flowers are mainly upright (few are pendant) and are sold by the stem. The most popular varieties include 'Enchantment' (orange), 'Connecticut King' (yellow) and 'Sterling Star' (white).

ORIENTAL HYBRIDS (sometimes called trumpet lilies): Cup-shaped with recurved petals, generally pendant, up to 8 in (20 cm) across, with only 1-3 flowers per stem. The main varieties include 'Journey's End' (pink), 'Star Gazer' (upright pink) and 'Laura-Lee' (pink). They are usually sold per stem.

SPECIOSUM LILIES: The flowers open up flat, with the petal tips recurved, measure 5-6 in (12-16 cm) across, with 6-9 hanging flowers per stem. The main varieties include 'Album' (white), 'Ushida' (pink with white edge) and 'Rubrum' (pink).

Similar in shape to these lilies only smaller and with more recurved petals is the orange tiger lily (*L. tigrinum*).

EASTER LILIES: Usually 5-7 in (12-18 cm) long. The trumpet-shaped flowers grow sideways, and there are generally 1-6 flowers per stem. They are usually sold per flower, not stem.

All the varieties in this group have been developed from *L. longiflorum*.

AURATUM LILIES: The largest flowers of all the lilies, with pendulous white flowers with orange stripes and red flecks. They are usually sold per flower, not stem.

TIME TO BUY: When all the flowers on the stem are in bud stage, but the majority of them are clearly showing good colour. Buds that do not show colour usually do not open once cut. Special care should be taken in the early winter months to purchase 'ripe' lilies, since lilies may have been grown without artificial lighting, which may result in buds dropping before they open.

AVAILABILITY: All year round, but mainly late spring and summer.

VASE LIFE: 10-14 days, during which time the flowers continue to open up.

SPECIAL HOME CARE: Remove the lower white section of the stem that does not take in water well. Add only a small dose of flower food to the water: a larger dose may encourage yellowing of the leaves. Lily leaves tend to die before the flowers do, and these, as well as wilting flowers, are best removed. Some types of lilies (such as the speciosum types) are more prone to premature yellowing of the leaves.

The pollen of lilies stains clothing (especially suede). The flower is not harmed if the stamens are snipped off with scissors.

TRADE CARE: Best kept cooled at 36-41°F (2-5°C).

At these temperatures they can be kept for a maximum of 2-3 days without water. Prolonged dry storage of lilies can cause browning and curling of petal tips, and result in a short vase life — damage that is not apparent until they have opened up. In water, at cooled temperatures, lilies can be held for 4-5 days, during which time they will begin to open up. Bud development can be affected if lilies are kept for a prolonged time at temperatures below 41°F (5°C). Easter lilies are best kept at slightly lower temperatures, 32-36°F (0-2°C).

Asiatic hybrids are the only lilies that are sensitive to ethylene gas damage.

Finally, handle the flowers very carefully since they bruise easily.

LILY-OF-THE-VALLEY
Convallaria

FAMILY: Liliaceae

BOTANICAL NAME: *Convallaria majalis*

DESCRIPTION: Small, white or pink, bell-shaped nodding flowers are borne in loose, often one-sided clusters. Arching stems usually carry 6-8 loose, often one-sided clusters. Stem length is usually no more than 8-10 in (20-25 cm). There are single forms, such as 'Fortin's Giant' (white) and 'Rosea' (pink) and double forms, such as 'Plena' (white). Single white forms are the most popular.

TIME TO BUY: When the bells are well developed. If the terminal flower is deep green, the flowers have been harvested too soon and may not open up.

AVAILABILITY: Spring.

VASE LIFE: 4-6 days.

TRADE CARE: Can be kept for 2-3 weeks at 30-32°F (−1-0°C), as long as the rhizome is attached. Once cut, temperatures between 36-37°F (2-3°C) are suitable, but should be placed in water immediately.

These flowers wilt quickly if exposed to heat or poor air circulation.

SUITABLE FOR DRYING

LINARIA
Toadflax

Linaria purpurea

FAMILY: Scrophulariaceae
BOTANICAL NAME: *Linaria purpurea*
DESCRIPTION: Related to and resembling snap-dragons, the flowers are less than 1in (2.5 cm) long and appear in spikes. The stems, when cut, are 24-28in (60-70 cm). The flowers are usually bi-coloured, in purple or pink.
TIME TO BUY: When the first florets on the spike have already opened.
AVAILABILITY: Late summer to autumn.
VASE LIFE: Up to 10 days.
SPECIAL HOME CARE: Keep away from fruit, vegetables, excess heat, and damaged or wilting flowers.
TRADE CARE: Best kept cooled at 36-41°F (2-5°C). Storage is not recommended. Susceptible to ethylene gas damage.

LISIANTHUS
Wildflower, Prairie gentian

FAMILY: Gentianaceae
BOTANICAL NAME: *Eustoma grandiflorum*
DESCRIPTION: Anemone-shaped, cupped flowers, 1½in (4cm) across, appear at the end of branchlets that stem from a 16-20in (40-50 cm) long stem. There are usually 3-5 flowers that open on a stem. The main colours are white, such as 'Snowball' and 'Double White', lavender, such as 'Light Lavender', purple, such as 'Double Purple' and pink, such as 'Double Pink'.
TIME TO BUY: At least one of the flowers on the stem should be open, and a few of the buds starting to show colour.
AVAILABILITY: All year round.
VASE LIFE: 1-2 weeks.
SPECIAL HOME CARE: Keep away from excess heat and from direct sunlight. Re-cut the stems frequently.
TRADE CARE: Best kept at 36-41°F (2-5°C). In these conditions they can be held up to 2-3 days without water; in water, they can be held for up to 3 days.

LOBELIA

Lobelia fulgens

FAMILY: Campanulaceae
BOTANICAL NAME: *Lobelia* species
DESCRIPTION: Tubular flowers appear along a spike, 12 in (30 cm) long. The flowers come mainly in shades of red. The stem, when cut, is usually 18-22 in (45-55 cm) long. From *L. fulgens*, 'Queen Victoria' is deep red and 'Bee's Flame' is scarlet; *L. syphilitica* is blue.
TIME TO BUY: When the first buds on the spike are showing colour but before they open — once one flower is open, the rest of the buds develop very quickly.
AVAILABILITY: Mainly autumn and early winter.
VASE LIFE: 7-10 days.
TRADE CARE: Best kept cooled, at 36-41°F (2-5°C). They can be held in water for 2-4 days. Dry storage is not recommended.

LONAS

FAMILY: Compositae
BOTANICAL NAME: *Lonas inodora*
DESCRIPTION: The terminal flower heads measure 2 in (5 cm) across, and consist of small yellow flowers grouped into a tight cluster. The overall length, when cut, is no more than 12 in (30 cm).
TIME TO BUY: When the flowers are just starting to open.
AVAILABILITY: Summer.
VASE LIFE: Approximately 1 week.
TRADE CARE: Best kept at 36-41°F (2-5°C). Storage is not recommended.
SUITABLE FOR DRYING

LUPINUS
Lupin

Lupinus 'Royal Parade', Russell hybrid

FAMILY: Leguminosae
BOTANICAL NAME: *Lupinus polyphyllus* hybrids, especially the Russell strains
DESCRIPTION: Thin stems are densely covered with pea-shaped flowers, forming flower spikes up to 24 in (60 cm) in length. The overall length of the stem and flower spike, when cut, is usually 24-32 in (60-80 cm). The flowers come in a wide variety of colours, and are usually bi-coloured.
TIME TO BUY: When the majority of the flowers on the spike have begun to open.
AVAILABILITY: Summer.
VASE LIFE: Approximately 1 week.
TRADE CARE: Best kept at 36-41°F (2-5°C). Storage is not recommended.

LYSIMACHIA

FAMILY: Primulaceae
BOTANICAL NAME: *Lysimachia* species
DESCRIPTION: Small, star-shaped flowers are densely packed in 4 in (10 cm) spikes. The stems, when cut, reach up to 28 in (70 cm) in length. *Lysimachia*

clethroides has white flowers; *Lysimachia punctata* has larger, yellow flowers.
TIME TO BUY: When flowers are starting to open.
AVAILABILITY: Summer.
VASE LIFE: Approximately 1 week.
SPECIAL HOME CARE: Keep away from direct sunlight and excess heat to avoid dehydration of the flowers.
TRADE CARE: Best kept cooled, at 36-41°F (2-5°C). Storage is not recommended.

MAHONIA

Mahonia aquifolium

FAMILY: Berberidaceae
BOTANICAL NAME: *Mahonia japonica*
DESCRIPTION: Small, yellow flowers form dense, often drooping panicles, 3-5 in (8-12 cm) long. The stems, when cut, are usually over 24 in (60 cm) in length.
TIME TO BUY: When in bud, but clearly showing colour.
AVAILABILITY: Winter.
VASE LIFE: Approximately 1 week.
TRADE CARE: Best kept at 36-50°F (5-10°C). Place in water as soon as possible. Storage is not recommended.

MALOPE

Malope trifida

FAMILY: Malvaceae
BOTANICAL NAME: *Malope trifida*
DESCRIPTION: Wide trumpet-shaped flowers 2-3 in (5-8 cm) across, appear in terminal clusters on stems that are 24-28 in (60-70 cm) when cut. The flowers come in shades of pink and purple with veined petals; white varieties, though less common, are also found.
TIME TO BUY: When the flowers start to open.
AVAILABILITY: Summer.
VASE LIFE: 5-7 days.
TRADE CARE: Best kept at 36-41°F (2-5°C). Storage is not recommended.

MALVA
Mallow

Malva alcea

Closely related and similar to lavatera. Both flower types are commonly known as mallow.
FAMILY: Malvaceae
BOTANICAL NAME: *Malva alcea*
DESCRIPTION: Funnel-shaped flowers, 2 in (5 cm) across, appear on spikes. The main colours are white, and shades of pink. The stem, when cut, is 24-32 in (60-80 cm) long.
TIME TO BUY: When the flowers start to open.
AVAILABILITY: Summer.
VASE LIFE: Approximately 1 week.
TRADE CARE: Best kept at 36-41°F (2-5°C). Storage is not recommended.

MIMOSA
Acacia, Wattle

FAMILY: Leguminosae
BOTANICAL NAME: *Acacia dealbata*
DESCRIPTION: Minute, petal-less, fluffy, yellow flowers appear in profusion in terminal panicles. The woody stems, when cut, are no more than 16-20 in (40-50 cm) long. The flowers are fragrant.

There are more than 100 varieties, of which only a few are commercialised as cut flowers. The main ones include: 'Floribunda', 'Gaullois', 'Mirandole', 'Monteana', 'Turner' (or 'Tournaire') and 'Banana'.
TIME TO BUY: Two types of mimosa are available: green mimosa, which is the earlier, unopen stage, and yellow mimosa, which has open flowers.
Green mimosa is sold accompanied by an opening crystal, but rarely flowers to its full capacity.
Yellow mimosa should be bought when the majority of the flowers have begun to open. Once mimosa has begun to open, its flowering time is short, so care should be taken not to buy yellow mimosa in too developed a stage.
VASE LIFE: 5-6 days.
SPECIAL HOME CARE: Re-cut at least 2 in (5 cm) off the end of the stem. These are woody, so use secateurs; do not crush the stems. Keep mimosa away from excess heat, direct sunlight, fruits, vegetables and damaged or wilting flowers.
TRADE CARE: Best kept cooled, at 36-41°F (2-5°C) — and can be kept as low as 30-36° (−1-2°C). Under these conditions, green mimosa can be kept for as long as 1 week, and yellow mimosa for 3-4 days in water. Green mimosa should be put into water with the opening crystal that is usually sold with it. Storage without water is not recommended for more than 2 days.
If green mimosa suffers any drastic changes of temperature from the time it was picked, the flowers may not open up well — a factor not always in control of the receiver — hence the drop in popularity of green mimosa.
Mimosa is sensitive to ethylene gas damage.
Mimosa is generally sold by weight, in bunches of 5 oz, 8 oz or 1 lb (150, 250 or 500 g).
SUITABLE FOR DRYING

MOLUCCELLA
Bells of Ireland, Shell flower

FAMILY: Labiatae
BOTANICAL NAME: *Moluccella laevis*
DESCRIPTION: The small, white, fragrant flowers are surrounded by a large, shell-like green calyx. They appear along an 8-12 in (20-30 cm) long spike, on stems that average 20-32 in (50-80 cm) in length.
TIME TO BUY: When the flowers are open.
They are generally sold with the leaves of the spike stripped off so that the flowers are clearly visible.

AVAILABILITY: Mainly spring.

VASE LIFE: 8-10 days.

SPECIAL HOME CARE: Keep away from excess heat and direct sunlight. Cut stems frequently, to prevent drooping of the spike tip.

TRADE CARE: Best kept cooled, at 36-41°F (2-5°C). In these conditions, they can be held for up to 4 days in water. Dry storage is not recommended.

SUITABLE FOR DRYING

MONARDA
Bergamot

Monarda didyma

FAMILY: Labiatae

BOTANICAL NAME: *Monarda didyma*

DESCRIPTION: The flowers, 2-3in (5-8cm) across, appear in dense heads of red, purple or pink. They appear singly at the end of the stem or in twin whorls on the stem. The overall length, when cut, is over 24in (60cm).

AVAILABILITY: Summer.

TIME TO BUY: When the flowers are starting to open.

VASE LIFE: Approximately 1 week.

TRADE CARE: Best kept at 36-41°F (2-5°C). Storage is not recommended.

MUSCARI
Grape hyacinth

FAMILY: Liliaceae

BOTANICAL NAME: *Muscari armeniacum, M. botryoides*

DESCRIPTION: Tiny, tubular blue or white flowers appear densely clustered on terminal spikes. The stems are no more than 6in (15cm) long. The blue flowers generally have white rims.

TIME TO BUY: When only a few of the lower florets have started to open.

VASE LIFE: 4-6 days.

SPECIAL HOME CARE: Keep away from excess heat and direct sunlight.

TRADE CARE: Best kept at 36-41°F (2-5°C). At this temperature they can be held without water for 2-3 days.

SUITABLE FOR DRYING

NARCISSUS
Daffodils, Narcissus

Although all the varieties listed below are botanically narcissus, the single, trumpet-shaped flowers are known as daffodils, and the other varieties are known as narcissus or jonquils.

FAMILY: Amaryllidaceae

BOTANICAL NAME: *Narcissus* species

DESCRIPTION: Cup- or trumpet-shaped flowers that vary in colour and size, according to the variety. Single-flowered stems are 12-20in (30-50cm) long; multi-flowered stems are usually shorter. Narcissi, as cut flowers, can be divided according to their shape and size.

DAFFODIL, SINGLE-FLOWERED STEM: The corolla can be cup- or trumpet-shaped, and can be longer than the surrounding petals (trumpet), same size (cup) or shorter (as in Poeticus types, such as 'Actaea'). The traditional daffodil is yellow (such as 'Dutch Master' and 'Golden Harvest'). Other popular varieties include: yellow with orange centre (such as 'Fortune' and 'Hollywood'), white with orange centre (such as 'Sempre Avanti'), white with yellow centre (such as 'Jules Verne') and white (such as 'Ice Follies').

DOUBLE NARCISSUS, SINGLE-FLOWERED STEM: Can be yellow (such as 'Texas'), white with yellow centre (such as 'White Lion'), or white with orange centre (such as 'Flower Drift').

SMALL SINGLE NARCISSUS, MULTI-FLOWERED STEM: Can be yellow with orange centre (such as

'Geranium'), yellow (such as 'Soleil D'Or') or white (such as 'Paper White'). The flowers are small (no more than 1-1¼in (2.5-3cm) across), and very fragrant.

SMALL DOUBLE NARCISSUS, MULTI-FLOWERED STEM: Yellow with orange centre (such as 'Cheerfulness').
TIME TO BUY: The single-flowered, large narcissus (daffodils) should be bought when they are closed, with no or very little colour showing. The buds should be bent, and the buds' cuticles should have already split. This is commonly referred to as pencil or goose neck stage.

Double-flowered narcissus or multi-flowers on a stem should be bought when the flowers have just begun to open.
AVAILABILITY: Winter and spring.
VASE LIFE: 4-6 days.
SPECIAL HOME CARE: The latex given out by daffodils and narcissus is harmful to other flowers. They can usually only be mixed with other flowers if they have been allowed to stand in water on their own for 24 hours, and the water changed. However, a new preservative solution has come on the market that allows fresh daffodils to be mixed with other flowers.
TRADE CARE: Best kept at 36-41°F (2-5°C).

Daffodils can be kept, if in pencil stage, for up to 7 days at approximately 34°F (1°C). They are best kept lying flat in the boxes, without water. As soon as they are placed in water, or the temperature rises, they will begin to flower. Narcissus types can be held for only 2-3 days, dry, at 34°F (1°C).

All narcissus flowers will curve towards the light. They should be placed either in complete darkness or with light directly on top of them. To straighten curved narcissus stems, wrap them tightly in wet paper, and place in water under direct light.

NERINE
Guernsey lily

FAMILY: Amaryllidaceae
BOTANICAL NAME: *Nerine* species
DESCRIPTION: The flowers are composed of six, narrow, strap-shaped petals that are often crumpled and twisted. An average of 6-12 flowers forms a flower head 4-6in (10-16cm) across, at the end of a leafless stem that is 16-28in (40-70cm) when cut. The colours range from deep red through to bright pink and white.

N. bowdenii, *N. sarniensis* and *N. flexuosa* are the main species for cut flowers, that include the varieties 'Corusca Major' (red), 'Pink Triumph' (pink), 'Alba' (white). *Nerine crispa*, correctly *N. undulata*, is a smaller variety (shorter stem and smaller flowers) with crisped petals. *Amarine* is a hybrid between *Amaryllis* and *Nerine*, with larger flowers than those of a *Nerine*.
TIME TO BUY: When the flowers are starting to open. Buds that are not well developed will not open.
AVAILABILITY: Late summer to end of winter months
VASE LIFE: 10-14 days.
TRADE CARE: Best kept at 41-47°F (5-8°C). Lower temperatures may stop flower development and can cause frost damage. They can be held without water for 4-5 days.

NICOTIANA
Tobacco plant

Nicotiana alata

FAMILY: Solanaceae
BOTANICAL NAME: *Nicotiana alata*
DESCRIPTION: 3in (8cm) long, tubular flowers, mainly white, although also available in shades of cream, pink, red, purple and yellow. The flowers appear in clusters, at the end of stems that, when cut, reach 20-38in (50-70cm) in length.
TIME TO BUY: When the flowers have already started to open.

AVAILABILITY: Mainly spring.
VASE LIFE: Approximately 1 week.
TRADE CARE: Best kept at 36-41°F (2-5°C). Storage is not recommended.

NIGELLA
Love-in-a-mist

FAMILY: Ranunculaceae
BOTANICAL NAME: *Nigella damascena*
DESCRIPTION: Saucer-shaped flowers, 1-1¼in (2.5-3cm) across, are mainly grey-blue although pink, white and mauve varieties also exist. They appear in quantities at the end of thin stems that are between 16-18in (40-60cm) in length. The seed heads are attractive.
TIME TO BUY: When the majority of the flowers have begun to open but the petals are not yet separated from the centre.
AVAILABILITY: Mainly summer.
VASE LIFE: 1 week to 10 days.
SPECIAL HOME CARE: Frequent changing of water is recommended, as the water is quickly polluted.
TRADE CARE: Best kept cooled, at 36-41°F (2-5°C). Storage is not recommended.
SUITABLE FOR DRYING

ODONTOGLOSSUM

Odontoglossum Royal Wedding 'Cooksbridge'

FAMILY: Orchidaceae
BOTANICAL NAME: *Odontoglossum* species
DESCRIPTION: Erect spray of small, 2-2¾in (5-7cm) orchid flowers, on a single stem that, when cut, averages 20in (50cm) in length. The flowers have wide open petals and sepals, resulting in a flat appearance. They are usually conspicuously bi-coloured (mainly white, pink and pale yellow, with brown or red spotting), and often have crisped petals.
TIME TO BUY: At least half of the buds on the spray should be fully opened.
AVAILABILITY: All year round.
VASE LIFE : 10 days to 2 weeks.
SPECIAL HOME CARE: See Special Care for Orchids, Chapter 1.
TRADE CARE: See Special Care for 'Tropical' Flowers, Chapter 7.

ONCIDIUM
Golden shower

FAMILY: Orchidaceae
BOTANICAL NAME: *Oncidium splendidum, O. variocos*
DESCRIPTION: Masses of small, ¾in (2cm) wide, yellow orchid flowers appear on long, thin stems that arch with the weight of the flowers. The stem length is usually 24in (60cm).
TIME TO BUY: When most of the flowers on the spray have already opened.
AVAILABILITY: All year round.
VASE LIFE: 10 days to 2 weeks.
SPECIAL HOME CARE: See Special Care for Orchids, Chapter 1.
TRADE CARE: See Special Care for 'Tropical' Flowers, Chapter 7.

ORNITHOGALUM
Chincherinchee, Star of Bethlehem, Windlily

FAMILY: Liliaceae
BOTANICAL NAME: *Ornithogalum* species
DESCRIPTION: White, star-shaped flowers, 1¼in (3cm) wide when open, appear in a tight cluster at the end of a leafless stem. The cluster of flowers measures up to 4-5in (10-12cm) long, and the total stem length when cut varies between 16-24in (40-60cm).

Ornithologalum thyrsoides is the main species for cut flowers. The double and giant varieties 'Mont Blanc' and 'Mount Everest', are hybrids. They can all be tinted in pastel colours.

O. arabicum differs from *O. thyrsoides* in that the flower head is more spherical, the stem longer and thicker, and the small florets have a black centre.

TIME TO BUY: Approximately one-third of the florets should show colour when bought. The lower 1-2 flowers should have begun to open. Look out for yellowing stems, which indicate the flowers have been kept too long, and will not open.

AVAILABILITY: Mainly spring.

VASE LIFE: Over 2 weeks, during which time the flowers will continue to open up.

SPECIAL HOME CARE: Pinch off the top bud in order to promote better opening of the rest of the buds. Keep the flowers away from excess heat, and from fruit, vegetables and any decaying flowers.

TRADE CARE: Best kept at 36-41°F (2-5°C). At 36°F (2°C) they can be kept for up to 7 days without water.

Ornithogalums will curve towards light, so keep them either in the dark or with a light directly over them. They are sensitive to ethylene gas damage.

SUITABLE FOR DRYING (mainly 'Mont Blanc')

PARANOMUS

Paranomus reflexus

FAMILY: Proteaceae

BOTANICAL NAME: *Paranomus* species

DESCRIPTION: Loose spikes, up to 4 in (10 cm) long, that consist of small, woolly, yellow or pink flowers. The spike appears at the top of the woody stem that varies in length according to the variety.

Of the 18 species available, only a few are plentiful as cut flowers. These include: *P. bracteolaris*, *P. dregei* (both pink) and *P. reflexus* (yellow).

TIME TO BUY: When the flowers are already open, as they rarely continue to develop once cut.

AVAILABILITY: All year round.

VASE LIFE: Paranomus are quite hardy — approximately 10-15 days. No special care is required.

TRADE CARE: Best kept at 36-41°F (2-5°C). At these temperatures they can be held for 5-6 days without water. At room temperature, place in water as soon as possible.

SUITABLE FOR DRYING

PAEONIA
Peony

FAMILY: Ranunculaceae

BOTANICAL NAME: *Paeonia lactiflora* hybrids

DESCRIPTION: Solitary, terminal flower, single or double, that varies in shape from tubular to global, and measures approximately 2¾-5 in (7-12 cm) across.

Peonies can be divided into single, anemone-flowered (Japanese) and double forms.

TIME TO BUY: When still in bud, but clearly showing colour. The time of buying is critical as, once open, peonies have a short vase life.

AVAILABILITY: Spring and early summer.

VASE LIFE: If bought in bud stage, up to 10 days; if bought already open, approximately 5 days.

TRADE CARE: Best kept cooled at all times, at 36-41°F (2-5°C). If in bud stage, they can be held in dry storage for up to 10 days at 32°F (0°C). Once they are placed in water at room temperature they will begin to open up.

SUITABLE FOR DRYING

PHALAENOPSIS
Amabilis, Moth orchid

Phalaenopsis 'Red Lips'

FAMILY: Orchidiaceae
BOTANICAL NAME: *Phalaenopsis* hybrids
DESCRIPTION: The orchid flowers, 4 in (10 cm) across, come in yellow, violet, pink, white and blue, with rounded petals and sepals. There are up to 15 flowers (usually less) on thin, arching stems, which vary in length. *P. amabilis* is white, and *P. schilleriana* (commonly referred to also as *amabilis*) is pink.
TIME TO BUY: When the flowers are open.
AVAILABILITY: All year round.
VASE LIFE: Approximately 1 week.
SPECIAL HOME CARE: They are delicate flowers, that require careful handling as they bruise easily. Frequent re-cutting of the stem ends, addition of flower food, frequent changing of water and misting of the flowers are recommended to keep the moisture level high and to avoid flower drop. Keep away from draughts, excess heat, fruit, vegetables and decaying flowers.
TRADE CARE: See Special Care for 'Tropical' Flowers, Chapter 7.

PHLOX

FAMILY: Polemoniaceae
BOTANICAL NAME: *Phlox* hybrids
DESCRIPTION: Clusters of small, salver-shaped flowers appear amidst mid-green lanceolate leaves, at the end of stems that measure 16-24 in (40-60 cm) long. The flowers are mainly white, purple or pink.

Hybrids of *P. paniculata* such as the white 'White Admiral' and 'Rembrandt', and of *P. maculata* the pink variety 'Alpha'.
TIME TO BUY: When the majority of the flowers have opened. Do not buy if no flowers have opened.
AVAILABILITY: Summer and autumn.
VASE LIFE: Approximately 1 week.
SPECIAL HOME CARE: Sear the end of the stem with a flame or immerse in boiling water for a few seconds. This stops latex loss that causes premature wilting.
TRADE CARE: Best kept at 36-41°F (2-5°C), although nearer to 41°F (5°C) is recommended. Phlox does not last at all well without water. Storage is not recommended.

PHYSOSTEGIA
Obedient plant

FAMILY: Labiatae
BOTANICAL NAME: *Physostegia virginiana*
DESCRIPTION: 5 in (12 cm) long spikes with closely-set, small pink, white and mauve flowers, on stems that, when cut, reach 16-24 in (40-60 cm) in length.

The main varieties include *P. virginiana* (pink) and *P. virginiana* 'Summer Snow' (white).
TIME TO BUY: When the lower florets have opened.
AVAILABILITY: Summer.
VASE LIFE: Approximately 1 week.
TRADE CARE: Best kept at 36-41°F (2-5°C). Storage is not recommended.

POPPY
Papaver

Papaver nudicaule

FAMILY: Papaveraceae
BOTANICAL NAME: *Papaver nudicaule* (known as Iceland poppy); *Eschscholzia californica* (known as California poppy)
DESCRIPTION: Four, broad, overlapping petals, of a papery texture, forming a cup shape that opens up almost flat. The wiry stems, when cut, reach up to 24 in (60 cm). The flowers come in shades of pink, red, yellow and white and reach 2¾ in (7 cm) across when open.

The main varieties used for cut flowers are the biennial *P. nudicaule* and the annual *Eschscholzia californica*. The California poppy, a related species to the Iceland poppy, is similar in shape but the flowers are smaller.
TIME TO BUY: When the petals are just starting to break open.
AVAILABILITY: Summer and autumn.
VASE LIFE: 5-7 days.
SPECIAL HOME CARE: The stem ends should be seared with a flame or placed in boiling water for a few seconds, to stop loss of latex that will cause premature wilting of the flower.
TRADE CARE: Best kept at 36-41°F (2-5°C). 41°F (5°C) is recommended, although for short periods 36-39°F (2-4°C) will not harm the flowers. They do not last without water. The flowers should be unpacked and loosened up as soon as possible, as the thin stems tend to rot easily. Storage is not recommended.

PROTEA

For Pincushion proteas, see Leucospermum
FAMILY: Proteaceae
BOTANICAL NAME: *Protea* species
DESCRIPTION: Proteas consist of a flower surrounded by colourful bracts, usually cream or pink. The shape of the flower head can be coned or bowl-shaped. They stand usually singly at the end of woody stems that, when cut, average no more than 8-16 in (20-40 cm) in length. Some varieties have a silky brownish-red beard inside the bracts.

Amongst the long list of proteas, the main ones include: *P. cynaroides*, (king protea) up to 10 in (25 cm) across, pink, bowl-shaped; *P. magnifica* (queen protea), up to 8 in (20 cm) across, bowl-shaped, white or pink; *P. repens* (sugarbush or honeypot) small, cone-shaped flower, up to 6 in (15 cm) long, is red or white and is sticky to the touch; *P. grandiceps*, cone-shaped, up to 6 in (15 cm) across, with silky brown beard inside the bracts; *P. nerifolia* (pink mink), that is 5 in (12 cm) long, cone-shaped, with brown silky beard inside the bracts; and *P. compacta*, a 4 in (10 cm), cone-shaped flower that is pink or white.
TIME TO BUY: When the flower has developed but before the bracts have separated from the flower.
AVAILABILITY: All year round.
VASE LIFE: Up to 2 weeks.
SPECIAL HOME CARE: Re-cut the stem ends with secateurs; do not crush them. Frequent changes of water, addition of flower preservative to the water and frequent re-cutting of stems will lengthen the vase life, and delay the blackening of the leaves.
TRADE CARE: Although proteas are very hardy flowers that will remain for up to 3 weeks without signs of wilting, special care is required to take care of leaf blackening, a problem in all proteas but especially in *P. repens*, *P. compacta*, *P. magnifica* and *P. nerifolia*.

Proteas will keep for 1 week, dry, at 34-36°F (1-2°C). Proteas generate a lot of heat so maintaining a low temperature is vital. A high level of humidity should be accompanied by good air circulation so as to avoid the formation of fungus inside the flower heads.
SUITABLE FOR DRYING

PRUNUS

FAMILY: Rosaceae
BOTANICAL NAME: *Prunus* species
DESCRIPTION: Single or double flowers, 1-2 in (2.5-5 cm) across, appear along naked branches. When cut, the stems are usually 2-3 ft (60-100 cm) in length. The flowers are mainly white or pink.

The main cut flower varieties are: white flowering almond (*P. glandulosa* 'Albo-Plena'), pink almond (*P. triloba*), Japanese cherry (mainly hybrids), laurel blossom (*P. laurocerasus*) (white) and peach blossom (*P. persica*) (pink or white).

TIME TO BUY: When in bud stage, with a minimum of colour showing.
AVAILABILITY: Winter and early spring.
VASE LIFE: Over 2 weeks during which time the flowers will continue to open up.
SPECIAL HOME CARE: Prunus should be re-cut on arrival, using secateurs. Immersing the stem ends in boiling water for a few minutes will soften up the woody tissue, easing the flow of water up to the flower. The addition of preservative solution is strongly recommended to promote flowering. If possible, use preservative solutions specifically recommended for forcing shrubs.
TRADE CARE: As with other forcing shrubs, prunus can be kept in its dormant stage for up to a week at 30-32°F (−1-0°C) in a moist, dark atmosphere. Once in flower (or to promote flowering), keep in light, placed in water at 39-41°F (4-5°C). The water should contain forcing shrub preservative solution.

Prunus, as with all forcing shrubs, need a certain period of cold before the buds begin to open. In general, prunus bought before January can be stored in cold for longer than that bought later than January.

PYRETHRUM
Painted daisy

Pyrethrum roseum

FAMILY: Compositae
BOTANICAL NAME: *Pyrethrum roseum*
DESCRIPTION: Single and double forms of daisy-like flowers with a central yellow disc surrounded by petals that come in a wide variety of colours. The flowers are 2 in (5 cm) across, and the stem length is usually no more than 20 in (50 cm).

The main varieties used as cut flowers are hybrids, of which the most popular are the pink single varieties with yellow centre, e.g. 'Brenda'.

TIME TO BUY: The flowers should be starting to open.
AVAILABILITY: Mainly spring.
VASE LIFE: Over 1 week.
TRADE CARE: Best kept at 36-41°F (2-5°C). Under these conditions, they can be held for 2-4 days in water.

RANUNCULUS

Also known as Persian, French or Turban Buttercup
FAMILY: Ranunculaceae
BOTANICAL NAME: *Ranunculus asiaticus*

DESCRIPTION: These showy, bowl-shaped flowers resemble small peonies. There are single and double forms, they come in bright colours (yellow, orange, red and pink) and can vary in size from ¾-4 in (2-10 cm) in diameter. The hollow, brittle stems are 10-20 in (25-50 cm) in length when cut.

TIME TO BUY: When the flowers have started to open, but before the petals have separated from the centre.

AVAILABILITY: Late winter and early spring.

VASE LIFE: Up to 1 week.

SPECIAL HOME CARE: Avoid direct heat. If limp, place them in water, in a cool spot, tightly wrapped in paper, until they become sturdy.

TRADE CARE: Best kept at 36-41°F (2-5°C). Place in water as soon as possible. Storage is not recommended.

SUITABLE FOR DRYING

RESEDA
Mignonette

Reseda odorata

Also known as Peaches and Cream

FAMILY: Resedaceae

BOTANICAL NAME: *Reseda odorata*

DESCRIPTION: The flowers are ½ in (1 cm) across and are carried in loose heads. The main colour is greenish-yellow tinged with red, although red varieties also exist. The stems, when cut, are 24-28 in (60-70 cm) in length.

TIME TO BUY: When the flowers are already open.

AVAILABILITY: Summer and autumn

VASE LIFE: 8-10 days.

TRADE CARE: Best kept at 36-41°F (2-5°C). Storage is not recommended.

SUITABLE FOR DRYING

ROSE

FAMILY: Rosaceae

BOTANICAL NAME: *Rosa* hybrids

DESCRIPTION: Densely crowded petals in a variety of colours and sizes are borne on erect stems. The stem length, when cut, varies from 14 in (35 cm) to over 3 ft (1 m).

Roses as cut flowers can be divided as follows:

LARGE ROSES (mostly hybrid teas): The flower measures 4-6 in (10-15 cm) when open, and the stem length is 16-36 in (40-100 cm).

The main varieties include 'Visa', 'Madelon', 'Ilona' (red), 'Sonia', 'Pink Delight' (pink), 'Aalsmeer Gold', 'Cocktail 80' (yellow), 'White Masterpiece' (white).

MEDIUM-SIZE ROSES — SWEETHEART ROSES: The flower head measures from 2¾-4 in (7-10 cm) across when open, on stems that vary from 10-24 in (25-60 cm) in length.

The main varieties include 'Jaguar', 'Mercedes' (red), 'Golden Times' (yellow), 'Carol', 'Belinda' (pink), 'Champagne' (cream), 'Jack Frost' (white).

The name Sweetheart can cause confusion since it is sometimes used to refer to large roses, and sometimes to mini roses (following group).

SMALL (MINI) ROSES: The flower head is less than 2¾ in (7 cm) across, and the stem length is no more than 16 in (40 cm). These include: 'Red Garnette', 'Motrea' (red), 'Marimba' (pink).

SPRAY ROSES: Many small, 2-2¾ in (5-7 cm) across roses on a single stem. These include: 'Gloria Mundia' (red), 'Doris Rijkers' (pink).

TIME TO BUY: Before the petals have separated from the flower head. If in doubt, it is always best to buy a rose in a more developed rather than greener stage of openness. Roses cut too early may not open at all and have a tendency to 'neck' (bend at the flower base).

Generally, white roses can be bought at a later stage of development than pink and red cultivars.

AVAILABILITY: All year round.

VASE LIFE: About 2 weeks.

SPECIAL HOME CARE: Roses are tricky flowers to take care of. The main problem is keeping a clean and free flow of water up to the flower head. As soon as this flow is interrupted, the roses will bend at the base of the stem and droop. To ensure this good flow of water, re-cut the stems frequently, if possible underwater. Never crush the stem ends: this has been proved to reduce the vase life by as much as half.

Remove the lower leaves to conserve moisture. Removing the thorns will not harm the flower, as long as care is taken not to harm the bark.

A limp rose can sometimes be revived by immersing the entire flower in water for a few hours.

Keep the flowers away from excess heat and draughts.

TRADE CARE: Best kept at 36-41°F (2-5°C) although temperatures from 34-36°F (1-2°C) will not harm the flowers. At these low temperatures, and with a high humidity level, roses can be held for up to 4 days without water. Keep roses in water, at low temperatures, with the bunch wrapping on, as this helps prevent the necks from bending. (Bent necks are the result of weak roses, premature harvesting, or excessive water loss.)

SUITABLE FOR DRYING

RUDBECKIA
Cone flower

FAMILY: Compositae

BOTANICAL NAME: *Rudbeckia hirta*

DESCRIPTION: Daisy-like flower with petals surrounding a dark, cone-like centre. The flowers measure 3-4 in (8-10 cm) across, and the stems when cut reach 24-32 in (60-80 cm) in length. The petals are usually yellow; orange and purple are less common.

TIME TO BUY: When the flowers are starting to open.

AVAILABILITY: Summer and autumn.

VASE LIFE: 6-8 days.

SPECIAL HOME CARE: Keep away from direct sunlight and from excess heat. If the flowers look limp, wrap them tightly in wet paper, re-cut the stem ends and place them in water in a cool, dark spot until their stems become sturdy.

TRADE CARE: Best kept at 36-41°F (2-5°C). Storage is not recommended.

SALPIGLOSSIS
Painted tongue

Salpiglossis sinuata

FAMILY: Solanaceae

BOTANICAL NAME: *Salpiglossis sinuata*

DESCRIPTION: Funnel-shaped flowers, 2 in (5 cm) across, are multi-coloured in shades of red, orange, yellow and lavender. The petals have a velvety texture and are sticky to the touch. The stem ends are 16-24 in (40-60 cm) when cut.

TIME TO BUY: When the flowers are starting to open.

AVAILABILITY: Summer.

VASE LIFE: Approximately 1 week.

TRADE CARE: Best kept at 36-41°F (2-5°C). Storage is not recommended.

SALVIA

Salvia splendens

FAMILY: Labiatae
BOTANICAL NAME: *Salvia* species
DESCRIPTION: Tubular, two-lipped flowers, often hooded, appear in terminal racemes. The flowers are purple, pink, white or red and are ¾-2 in (2-5 cm) long. The stem, when cut, is over 20 in (50 cm) long.
TIME TO BUY: When the flowers are starting to open.
AVAILABILITY: Summer.
VASE LIFE: Approximately 1 week.
TRADE CARE: Best kept at 36-41°F (2-5°C). Storage is not recommended.

SAPONARIA
Outdoor Gypsophila

FAMILY: Caryophyllaceae
BOTANICAL NAME: *Saponaria officinalis, S. vaccaria* (now listed as *Vaccaria pyramidata*)
DESCRIPTION: Star-shaped flowers, ½-¾ in (1-2 cm) across, appear in profusion on branched stems, 20 in (50 cm) long and over. The flowers are pink or white.
TIME TO BUY: When the flowers are just starting to open.
AVAILABILITY: Summer.
VASE LIFE: Over 1 week.
SPECIAL HOME CARE: Keep away from fruit, vegetables, decaying flowers, and excess heat as these may cause premature flower drop and wilting.
TRADE CARE: Best kept at 36-41°F (2-5°C). Place in water as soon as possible. Storage is not recommended. They are sensitive to ethylene gas damage.

SCABIOSA
Scabious

Also known as Pincushion Flower
FAMILY: Dipsacaceae
BOTANICAL NAME: *Scabiosa caucasica, S. atropurpurea*
DESCRIPTION: Daisy-shaped flowers with large papery mauve or white petals surrounding a yellow centre. The flowers are 2 in (5 cm) across, and stand singly at the end of slender stems that are 20-28 in (50-70 cm) in length.
TIME TO BUY: When the flowers are starting to open.
AVAILABILITY: Mainly summer.
VASE LIFE: Scabiosas are delicate flowers, with a short vase life of 5-6 days.
SPECIAL HOME CARE: Keep away from direct sunlight, draughts and excess heat. Frequent re-cutting of the stems is recommended.
TRADE CARE: Best kept at 36-41°F (2-5°C). Place in water as soon as possible. Storage is not recommended.

SCHIZANTHUS
Butterfly flower

Schizanthus pinnatus

SCHIZOSTYLIS
Kaffir lily

Schizostylis coccinea

FAMILY: Solanaceae
BOTANICAL NAME: *Schizanthus pinnatus*
DESCRIPTION: Orchid-like flowers, 1½in (4cm) that are pink, purple and yellow, with marks or spots. They appear in profusion on stems that are 2ft (60cm) and over when cut.
TIME TO BUY: When the flowers have already started to open.
AVAILABILITY: Summer.
VASE LIFE: Approximately 1 week.
TRADE CARE: Best kept at approximately 41°F (5°C). Storage is not recommended.

The name Kaffir lily is sometimes used for clivias
FAMILY: Tridaceae
BOTANICAL NAME: *Schizostylis coccinea*
DESCRIPTION: 6-10, bright red or pink flowers, about 1½in (4cm) across, appear at the end of a 20-28in (50-70cm) long stem. The flowers are star-shaped.
TIME TO BUY: When a couple of flowers are clearly showing colour and are starting to open.
AVAILABILITY: Autumn.
VASE LIFE: Up to 10 days-2 weeks.
SPECIAL HOME CARE: Remove the lower, white section when re-cutting the stem. Keep away from fruit, vegetables, damaged flowers and excess heat, as these can promote premature wilting.
TRADE CARE: Best kept at 36-41°F (2-5°C); temperatures as low as 32-36°F (0-2°C) are sometimes recommended. In cooled conditions they can be held for 3-5 days dry. Once in water they will begin to open up. They are sensitive to ethylene gas damage.

SCILLA
Squill

FAMILY: Liliaceae
BOTANICAL NAME: *Scilla sibirica*
DESCRIPTION: 2-5 small flowers appear at the end of thin, short stems that are no more than ½-¾in (1-2cm) long when cut. The main colour is brilliant blue, although some pink, purple and white varieties also exist.
TIME TO BUY: Only a few of the flowers should be open and the majority of the rest showing true colour.
AVAILABILITY: Early summer.
VASE LIFE: 7-10 days, during which time the flowers will continue to open.
TRADE CARE: Best kept at 36-41°F (2-5°C). In these conditions they can be kept for 3-4 days, dry.

SEDUM

FAMILY: Crassulaceae
BOTANICAL NAME: *Sedum spectabile* and hybrids
DESCRIPTION: Small star-shaped flowers, that appear in dense terminal panicles, come in various shades of yellow, pink, red and white. The clusters are 4-6in (10-15cm) across. The stems, when cut, are approximately 18-24in (40-50cm) long.
TIME TO BUY: When the majority of the florets on the cluster have begun to open.
AVAILABILITY: Spring and autumn.
VASE LIFE: Approximately 8 days.
TRADE CARE: Best kept at room temperature. Avoid excess heat. Storage is not recommended.

SERRURIA
Blushing bride

Serruria florida

FAMILY: Proteaceae
BOTANICAL NAME: *Serruria florida*
DESCRIPTION: Small, woolly flower surrounded by white bracts that are tinged with pink. The flower head is 3in (8cm) wide, and the stem is 12-16in (30-40cm) long. Other varieties less commonly used as cut flowers do not have bracts surrounding the flower head.
TIME TO BUY: When the flowers have already opened.
AVAILABILITY: Summer.
VASE LIFE: 7-10 days.
TRADE CARE: Best kept at cooled temperatures, 36-41°F (2-5°C). In these conditions they can be held for up to 3-4 days without water, although they should be placed in water as soon as possible.
SUITABLE FOR DRYING

SIDALCEA

Sidalcea malviflora

FAMILY: Malvaceae
BOTANICAL NAME: *Sidalcea malviflora*
DESCRIPTION: Widely funnel-shaped flowers in shades of pink and red, appear on 8 in (20 cm) long spikes. The flowers are 2 in (5 cm) across when open. The overall length is usually over 24 in (60 cm), when cut.
TIME TO BUY: When the flowers have started to open.
AVAILABILITY: Mainly summer.
VASE LIFE: These flowers have a short vase life of 4-6 days.
SPECIAL HOME CARE: Keep the flowers away from draughts. Sprinkle them with water frequently to maintain a high level of humidity.
TRADE CARE: Best kept at 36-41°F (2-5°C). Place in water as soon as possible. Storage is not recommended.

SOLIDAGO
Golden rod

FAMILY: Compositae
BOTANICAL NAME: *Solidago* species

DESCRIPTION: Tiny, yellow flowers form plumed clusters, that appear at the end of the stems that, when cut, reach over 28 in (70 cm) in length. There are many varieties of solidago, most of them similar to the eye but differing slightly in shape and in flowering period. The main varieties come from hybrids or from *S. canadensis* and *S. virgaurea* and include 'Praecox' and 'Strahlenkrone'.

× *Solidaster* is a hybrid between *Aster* and *Solidago*.
TIME TO BUY: When a few of the tiny florets are starting to open, but the overall colour of the spray is still green.
AVAILABILITY: Summer and autumn.
VASE LIFE: 10 days.
TRADE CARE: Can be held for up to 5 days without water, at temperatures between 36-41°F (2-5°C). Once they are placed in water they will begin to open.
SUITABLE FOR DRYING

SPATHIPHYLLUM

Spathiphyllum blandum

FAMILY: Araceae
BOTANICAL NAME: *Spathiphyllum*
DESCRIPTION: These flowers are similar to anthu-

riums, with a leaf-like spathe that is 3 in (8 cm) across, and a protruding spike. They are pure white, and the stem, when cut, is 20 in (50 cm) in length. A popular variety is the hybrid 'Mauna Loa'.

TIME TO BUY: When the flowers are open.

AVAILABILITY: All year round.

VASE LIFE: Approximately 2 weeks.

TRADE CARE: Best kept at 47-59°F (8-15°C). At lower temperatures they may suffer from frost damage; higher temperatures can cause premature wilting. They can be held for as long as 1 week-10 days without water.

They bruise easily, so treat with care.

STATICE
Limonium, Sea Lavender

FAMILY: Plumbaginaceae

BOTANICAL NAME: *Limonium* species

DESCRIPTION: Tiny, narrowly funnel-shaped flowers appear in loose clusters. The shape and colour is different according to the variety. The stem length varies between 16-28 in (40-70 cm).

The various types of statice differ in shape:

L. sinuatum, or notch leaf statice, is the traditional statice that comes in blue, white, yellow, orange, pink, salmon and lavender and consists of loose terminal panicles. The stem length varies between 16-28 in (40-70 cm). This variety is sometimes tinted. *L. bonduellii* is similar to *L. sinuatum* but has yellow flowers.

L. latifolium, German statice or statice gyp, has very small mauve flowers that appear in diffuse panicles.

L. incanum is generally called sea lavender. Erect 12 in (30 cm) long branched stems have very small white flowers with a reddish-purple corolla, giving an overall pink effect. 'Dumosum' is the best. This is also called sea foam statice.

L. suworowiti, or rat tail statice, consists of a 16 in (40 cm) long stem, and has small pink flowers densely packed in plume-shaped spikes. The stems have an interesting curved shape.

TIME TO BUY: When the individual clusters have most calyxes open and are showing colour.

AVAILABILITY: Mainly summer and autumn.

VASE LIFE: Up to 2 weeks. No special care is required.

TRADE CARE: Can be kept without water for 4-5 days, and in water for up to 2 weeks, in humid, cool temperatures. It should not be wet when stored as it may rot.

SUITABLE FOR DRYING

STEPHANOTIS
Madasgascar jasmine, Waxflower

Stephanotis floribunda

The name Waxflower is also used to refer to Leptospermum

FAMILY: Asclepiadaceae

BOTANICAL NAME: *Stephanotis floribunda*

DESCRIPTION: White, waxy, fragrant flowers, 2 in (5 cm) across, come in clusters of around 8 flowers. The flowers are tubular with five spreading, ovate-oblong lobes. Stephanotis flowers are usually sold stemless, the small flowers packed in airtight bags.

TIME TO BUY: When the flowers are open.

AVAILABILITY: Summer and early autumn.

VASE LIFE: Stephanotis flowers have a short vase life of 4-5 days.

TRADE CARE: Best kept at 36-41°F (2-5°C). At these temperatures, stephanotis flowers can be held for up to one week without water with high relative humidity. The crush-proof bags not only protect them from bruising, but maintain a high moisture level.

STOCK
Matthiola, Gillyflower

FAMILY: Crucifèrae

BOTANICAL NAME: *Matthiola incana*

DESCRIPTION: 1¼in (3 cm) wide double flowers appear in close clusters along 6-8 in (15-20 cm) of the stems. The overall length when cut is 12-28 in (30-70 cm). The main colours are white, red, pink, cream, purple or yellow. M. *incana* is the only variety used for cutting.

TIME TO BUY: When half (approximately 6-10 flowers) are open.

AVAILABILITY: Mainly spring and summer.

VASE LIFE: Up to 7 days.

SPECIAL HOME CARE: Stocks are reputed to have a short vase life, weak stems and to contaminate water rapidly — all of which is avoidable with proper care.

Re-cut the stem ends, making sure to remove the white, lower section. Any excess foliage should be removed. The addition of flower food, frequent re-cutting of stem ends, and placing the flowers away from direct sunlight, excess heat and draughts, have all proved effective at prolonging the vase life of stocks.

TRADE CARE: Best kept at 36-41°F (2-5°C). At these temperatures they can be held for up to 2 days without water, although placing them in water as soon as possible is strongly recommended. Hold stocks in the dark, to avoid stem elongation. Prolonged refrigeration can result in loss of fragrance. The addition of flower food is essential, as the water is easily contaminated, causing bacterial build-up that can clog up the stem.

STRELITZIA
Bird of Paradise

FAMILY: Musaceae

BOTANICAL NAME: *Strelitzia reginae*

DESCRIPTION: The flower head consists of a green-purple, boat-shaped and beaked bract, from which emerges a succession of long, keeled orange and blue flowers. These stand erect to give a crest appearance. The stem reaches up to 4 ft (120 cm) in length and has one flower head per stem.

TIME TO BUY: When the first flower is fully open.

AVAILABILITY: All year round.

VASE LIFE: 7-14 days.

SPECIAL HOME CARE: Handle with care, as the flowers drop off easily. Re-cutting the stems has proved effective at prolonging the vase life of these flowers. Keep away from draughts, direct sunlight and excess heat.

When the flower has faded, do not discard it: remove or pull back the old flower, and make a ¼in (2 cm) slit at the rear end of the pod, near the stem. Reach in with your thumb and carefully lever out the new blossoms. Hold the pod at the bottom, and gently pull up the new blossoms into a fan. To enhance the appearance of the flowers further, snip off the brown tip at the end of the pod, cutting a new V-shaped tip.

TRADE CARE: Best kept at 47-50°F (8-10°C). At these temperatures they can be held without water for no more than 4 days, with a high relative humidity of 90 to 94 per cent. Good air circulation is essential to prevent the base of the flower rotting and dropping off.

The flower heads are shipped, individually wrapped, to protect the flower. Remove the paper from around the flowers with care, as the flowers are easily damaged.

If the bloom is to be used outside the pod, as in a corsage, be sure to wipe off all the natural juices from the base of the stem, as this jelly-like substance has an offensive smell. Dust the end of the stem with talcum powder to soak up any excess.

Preservative solutions have no proven effect on the longevity of strelitzias, while re-cutting of stem ends has had good results. Research is being carried out to transport strelitzias in bud, rather than as flowers which are easily damaged. Opening solutions with 10 per cent sucrose have proved reasonably effective, but the trials are still continuing.

SWEET PEA
Lathyrus

Lathyrus odorata

FAMILY: Leguminosae
BOTANICAL NAME: *Lathyrus odoratus*, mainly Spencer varieties.
DESCRIPTION: Pea-shaped, delicate flowers, 1 in (2.5 cm) across, that have wing-like petals. The flowers are borne along and close to the thin stems, that are 16-20 in (40-50 cm) in length.
The main colours are white and shades of pink and purple. There are 5-7 flowers on one stem. They are fragrant.
TIME TO BUY: When the flowers have begun to open.
AVAILABILITY: Spring to summer.
VASE LIFE: Approximately 5-7 days.
TRADE CARE: Best kept at 36-41°F (2-5°C). At temperatures between 32-34°F (0-2°C) they can be held for 4-5 days without water. Temperatures below 32°F (0°C) will damage the petals. Prolonged refrigeration will reduce fragrance.
Silver treatment has proved effective in prolonging the life of this flower. It is sensitive to ethylene gas damage.

SWEET WILLIAM
Dianthus barbatus

FAMILY: Caryophyllaceae
DESCRIPTION: Densely packed, flattened heads, 2¾-5 in (7-12 cm) across, are formed by many small single or double flowers in mainly red, white, pink or purple. Many of the flowers are bi-coloured. The stems, when cut, are 20-28 in (50-70 cm) long.
TIME TO BUY: When the majority of the flowers on the cluster are starting to open. When buying sweet williams, look out for straight stems — curved stems cannot be straightened.
AVAILABILITY: Spring and summer.
VASE LIFE: 7-10 days.
SPECIAL HOME CARE: Keep away from fruit, vegetables, dying flowers and excess heat, that can encourage premature wilting.
TRADE CARE: Best kept at 36-41°F (2-5°C). Can be kept in controlled conditions for up to 5 days without water. They are sensitive to ethylene gas damage.
SUITABLE FOR DRYING

TAGETES
African marigold

Tagetes erecta

FAMILY: Compositae
BOTANICAL NAME: *Tagetes erecta*
DESCRIPTION: 2 in (5 cm) flowers that can be single (daisy-shaped) or more usually double (carnation-shaped). The flowers are mainly yellow or orange. The stem, when cut, is 24-32 in (60-80 cm) long.
TIME TO BUY: When the flowers are starting to open.
AVAILABILITY: Summer.
VASE LIFE: Over 1 week.
TRADE CARE: Best kept at 36-41°F (2-5°C). Storage is not recommended.
SUITABLE FOR DRYING

THALICTRUM
Meadow rue

Thalictrum aquilegifolium

FAMILY: Ranunculaceae
BOTANICAL NAME: *Thalictrum* species
DESCRIPTION: Open, tufted panicles, 6-8 in (15-20 cm) long, of fluffy white or purple flowers appear on long stems, 28 in (70 cm) and over. The panicles appear on branchlets, forming an overall large cluster at the end of the stem. *T. aquilegifolium* has denser panicles than *T. dipterocarpum*.
TIME TO BUY: When the majority of the flowers are starting to open.

AVAILABILITY: Early summer.
VASE LIFE: Approximately 1 week.
TRADE CARE: Best kept at 36-41°F (2-5°C). Storage is not recommended.

TRACHELIUM
Throatwort

FAMILY: Campanulaceae
BOTANICAL NAME: *Trachelium caeruleum*
DESCRIPTION: Clustered panicles of tiny flowers, usually purple, at the end of 20-28 in (50-70 cm) long stems. Pink varieties also exist but are less common.
TIME TO BUY: When only a few of the flowers on the cluster are starting to open.
AVAILABILITY: Summer.
VASE LIFE: 1 week to 10 days.
TRADE CARE: Best kept at 36-41°F (2-5°C). Storage is not recommended.
SUITABLE FOR DRYING

TRICYRTIS
Toad lily

FAMILY: Liliaceae
BOTANICAL NAME: *Tricyrtis macropoda*
DESCRIPTION: ¾ in (2 cm) long, bell-shaped flowers in varying shades of lavender, appear in groups at the end of 24-32 in (60-80 cm) long stems. The flowers are spotted with purple.
TIME TO BUY: When in bud, but already clearly showing colour.
AVAILABILITY: Summer and autumn.
VASE LIFE: 10 days, during which time they will continue to open
TRADE CARE: Best kept at 36-41°F (2-5°C). In these conditions can be held without water for a maximum of 3 days.

TRITONIA

Tritonia crocata

FAMILY: Iridaceae
BOTANICAL NAME: *Tritonia crocata*
DESCRIPTION: These flowers are similar to and closely related to freesia, ixia and crocosmia. Tritonias produce several shallow cup-shaped flowers, 1½in (4cm) wide, that appear in two ranks at the top of the stem. Main varieties are orange; pink and yellow varieties also exist. The stem length averages 16in (40cm).
TIME TO BUY: When the first florets are showing true colour, but have not yet opened.
AVAILABILITY: Mainly summer.
VASE LIFE: 5-7 days.
SPECIAL HOME CARE: When re-cutting the stems, remove the white, lower section. Keep away from fruit, vegetables, excess heat and dying flowers.
TRADE CARE: Best kept at 32-36°F (0-2°C). In these conditions, can be kept for up to 3 days without water. Once placed in water they will begin to open. They are sensitive to ethylene gas damage.

TROLLIUS
Globe Flower

Trollius 'Orange Princess'

FAMILY: Ranunculaceae
BOTANICAL NAME: *Trollius* species.
DESCRIPTION: Globe-shaped flowers, 2-2½in (5-6cm) across, that resemble buttercups. They are yellow or orange and stand on stems that are usually no more than 12-20in (30-50cm) long.
TIME TO BUY: When the petals are starting to separate from the centre.
AVAILABILITY: Early summer.
VASE LIFE: 5-7 days.
TRADE CARE: Best kept at 34-36°F (1-2°C). Storage is not recommended.

TUBEROSE
Polianthes

Polianthes tuberosa

TULIP

Tulipa 'Ajax' (single, rounded)

FAMILY: Amaryllidaceae (sometimes placed in Agavaceae).
BOTANICAL NAME: *Polianthes tuberosa*
DESCRIPTION: Pure white flowers, about 1in (2.5cm) across, appear closely together along erect spikes. Each flower has six open petals growing from a funnel-shaped tube. The stem, when cut, measures 24-32in (60-80cm) in length. Some varieties produce double flowers. They are very fragrant.
TIME TO BUY: When only the first flowers are starting to open, and most of them are showing colour.
AVAILABILITY: Mainly summer.
VASE LIFE: Up to 2 weeks, during which time they will continue to flower.
SPECIAL HOME CARE: The top bud is best removed to prevent stem curvature.
TRADE CARE: Best kept at 47-59°F (8-15°C). Below 43°F (6°C) can prevent proper opening of the flowers. They can be kept for as long as 3-4 days without water. Prolonged time in the cold room may reduce fragrance.

FAMILY: Liliaceae
BOTANICAL NAME: *Tulipa* species
DESCRIPTION: Single, goblet-shaped flowers with six petals, that vary from slender and pointed to broadly rounded. Only a few varieties are double, and all the varieties usually used for cut flowers have a single bloom per stem. The flowers, when fully mature, open up flat. Both stem length and size of bloom varies.

Botanically, tulips are classified into 15 divisions. As cut flowers, they can be grouped into four general categories, according to the shape of the flower.

There are hundreds of varieties of tulips, with new varieties coming out all the time. The main colours are red, yellow, orange, pink, purple and white, as well as bi-coloured.

SINGLE TULIP, ROUNDED PETALS: This is the most common variety, such as 'Appeldoorn' (red).
DOUBLE TULIP, ROUNDED PETALS: Such as 'Monte Carlo' (yellow).
PARROT TULIP, FRINGED PETAL, SINGLE FORM: Such as 'Flaming Parrot' (white/pink).
LILY-FLOWERED TULIP, POINTED PETALS, SINGLE FORM: Such as 'Aladdin' (red).

Tulipa 'Peach Blossom' (double, rounded)

Tulipa 'Aladdin' (lily-flowered)

Tulipa 'Estella Rijnveld' (parrot)

TIME TO BUY: When in a closed bud, but colour should be clearly showing. As a rule, the upper half should be coloured and the rest should still be green. Tulips that do not show any colour at all rarely open.

AVAILABILITY: Winter and spring.

VASE LIFE: Tulips are long-lasting flowers — 3-4 days in opening stage, and a further week open.

SPECIAL HOME CARE: Re-cut the stems, removing the white lower end of the stem; further re-cutting is not necessary. Tulips continue to grow for their first 24 hours in water. Addition of flower food to the water will promote full opening of the flower, and will keep the water in the vase clean and free of bacteria. Do not mix tulips with daffodils, unless the daffodils have been treated beforehand (see Narcissus).

Tulips curve towards light, so choose an evenly lit spot. If the stems are bent on arrival, they can be straightened by wrapping them tightly in wet paper and placing them in water, with light directly above them. Slitting or piercing the base of the flower to avoid curvature has no proven effects. Check the water level of the vase frequently, as tulips are 'heavy-drinkers'.

TRADE CARE: Best kept in a cold room 32-36°F (0-2°C). For short-term storage, the flowers should be re-cut and placed in water, tightly wrapped. To keep tulips for more than 5 days, they should be stored in a vertical position with no water — since once they are placed in water they will begin to open up. For longer than 10 days, tulips will only keep if they have their bulb attached.

Tulips and daffodils cannot be mixed together (see Narcissus).
SUITABLE FOR DRYING

VALERIAN

Valeriana officionalis

FAMILY: Valerianaceae
BOTANICAL NAME: *Valeriana sambusifolia*
DESCRIPTION: Small, tubular flowers form a 4-6 in (10-15 cm) flat cluster at the top of the stem, that when cut reaches 2 ft (60 cm) and over. The flowers are pink.
TIME TO BUY: When the flowers are already open.
AVAILABILITY: Beginning of summer.
VASE LIFE: 5-7 days.
TRADE CARE: Best kept at 36-41°F (2-5°C). Storage is not recommended.

VALLOTA
Scarborough lily

Vallota speciosa

FAMILY: Amaryllidaceae
BOTANICAL NAME: *Vallota speciosa*
DESCRIPTION: The 3-4 in (8-10 cm) flowers are funnel-shaped, and stand erect in groups of up to 10 flowers at the end of a stem that is 16-20 in (40-50 cm) long. The flowers are bright red.
TIME TO BUY: When a couple of flowers on the stem are starting to open, and the majority of flowers are showing colour.
AVAILABILITY: Mainly summer.
VASE LIFE: 10-14 days.
TRADE CARE: Best kept at 47-59°F (8-15°C). Below 43°F (6°C) can stop flower opening and cause frost damage to the petals. They can be held without water for up to 3-4 days. Once in water, they will begin to open up.

VANDA

VERBENA

Vanda coerulea

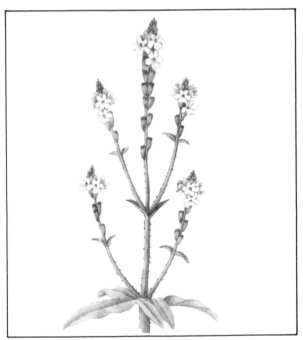

Verbena officinalis

FAMILY: Orchidaceae
BOTANICAL NAME: *Vanda* species
DESCRIPTION: Spray of up to 15 orchid flowers, 2¾-4 in (7-10 cm) across, have a shape similar to a pansy. The stems, when cut, are 24-32 in (60-80 cm) long. The main colour is blue, but orange, yellow, pink and white varieties also exist. Most varieties are shaded or spotted. *V. coerulea* is blue, and hybrids from *V. teres* and *V. tricolor* are white, or yellow-orange. A smaller variety, 'Miss Joaquim', has lavender petals and a blue centre.
TIME TO BUY: When the flowers are already open.
AVAILABILITY: All year round.
VASE LIFE: Up to 2 weeks.
SPECIAL HOME CARE: See Special Care for Orchids, Chapter 1.
TRADE CARE: See Special Care for 'Tropical' Flowers, Chapter 7.

FAMILY: Verbenaceae
BOTANICAL NAME: *Verbena bonariensis*
DESCRIPTION: Tight clusters of 2¾ in (7 cm) pink lavender flowers that are fragrant, and stand at the end of tall stems that are over 24 in (60 cm) in length.
TIME TO BUY: When the flowers are open.
AVAILABILITY: Summer through to autumn.
VASE LIFE: Approximately 1 week.
TRADE CARE: Best kept at 36-41°F (2-5°C). Storage is not recommended.
SUITABLE FOR DRYING

VERONICA

FAMILY: Scrophulariaceae
BOTANICAL NAME: *Veronica spicata*
DESCRIPTION: Terminal erect racemes, 2½-6 in (4-15 cm) long, composed of small purple flowers, appear on stems that are approximately 24 in (60 cm) in length. White varieties, less common, also exist.
TIME TO BUY: When the lower florets are already open.
AVAILABILITY: Summer
VASE LIFE: Approximately 1 week.
SPECIAL HOME CARE: Frequent re-cutting of stem ends can lengthen the vase life. Keep away from fruit, vegetables, dying flowers and excess heat.
TRADE CARE: Best kept at 36-41°F (2-5°C). Storage is not recommended. They are ethylene gas sensitive.

VIBURNUM

Snowball, Guelder rose

FAMILY: Caprifoliaceae
BOTANICAL NAME: *Viburnum opulus*
DESCRIPTION: Fragrant, tubular flowers from terminal flat heads that are 2-4 in (5-10 cm) or more across. The flowers are white, and stand on stems that are over 28 in (70 cm) when cut.
TIME TO BUY: When the overall colour is light green. The flowers will turn white as they open up.
AVAILABILITY: Late winter and spring.
VASE LIFE: 1 week to 10 days.
SPECIAL HOME CARE: The woody stems can be softened by immersing them for a few minute in boiling water. This will free the flow of water up the stem.
TRADE CARE: Best kept at 36-41°F (2-5°C). They should be kept in water.

VIOLA
Violet

Viola odorata

FAMILY: Violaceae
BOTANICAL NAME: *Viola odorata*
DESCRIPTION: Solitary, often nodding violet and white flowers, ¾ in (2 cm) across, come in single and double forms. The stems are no more than 6 in (15 cm) long.
TIME TO BUY: When the flowers are starting to open.
AVAILABILITY: Spring.
VASE LIFE: 3-6 days.
SPECIAL HOME CARE: Avoid heat and direct sunlight.
TRADE CARE: Best kept at 36-41°F (2-5°C). If kept at 30-32°F (−1-0°C), they can be held for up to 1 week. Prolonged refrigeration may reduce fragrance.

VUYLSTEKEARA
Cambria

Vuylstekeara 'Cambria Plush'

WATSONIA

Watsonia ardernei

FAMILY: Orchidaceae
BOTANICAL NAME: *Vuylstekeara* hybrids
DESCRIPTION: Spray of up to 9 flowers on a stem that, when cut, reaches 20-28 in (50-70 cm) in length. The main variety is 'Cambria Plush' with flowers 3-4 in (8-10 cm) across, which are red with a wide protruding white-red lip.
TIME TO BUY: When all, or most, of the flowers on the stem have opened.
AVAILABILITY: All year.
VASE LIFE: Up to 2 weeks.
SPECIAL HOME CARE: Keep away from fruit, vegetables, excess heat and dying flowers. Avoid draughts. If they look limp, they can often be revived by immersing them entirely in tepid water for a few minutes. Frequent misting of the flower heads is also recommended.
TRADE CARE: Best kept at 47-59°F (8-15°C). Lower temperatures may cause frost damage; higher temperatures will produce premature wilting. They are shipped with a water vial or wet cotton wool attached to the end of the stem. This should be removed within a week of shipping and replaced with fresh water. They are ethylene gas sensitive.

FAMILY: Iridaceae
BOTANICAL NAME: *Watsonia ardernei, W. coccinea*
DESCRIPTION: Slender stems, over 24 in (60 cm) in length, carry ¾-2 in (2-5 cm) wide flowers that are usually pink, six-petalled and star-shaped.
TIME TO BUY: When the lower flowers on the spike are just starting to open.
AVAILABILITY: Spring.
VASE LIFE: Over 1 week, during which time the flowers will continue to open.
SPECIAL HOME CARE: Keep away from fruit, vegetables, wilting flowers and excess heat.
TRADE CARE: Best kept at 36-41°F (2-5°C), although temperatures as low as 32°F (0°C) are also recommended. In these conditions, they can be held for up to 3-4 days without water. Once placed in water they will open up. They are sensitive to ethylene gas damage.

XERANTHEMUM
Paperflower

FAMILY: Compositae
BOTANICAL NAME: *Xeranthemum* species
DESCRIPTION: Solitary flower heads consist of numerous tiny white, pink or purple flowers. They appear at the end of branching stems that are over 20 in (50 cm) when cut.
TIME TO BUY: When most of the florets are open.
AVAILABILITY: Mainly summer.
VASE LIFE: 1 week.
TRADE CARE: Best kept at 36-41°F (2-5°C). Storage is not recommended.
SUITABLE FOR DRYING

YARROW
Achillea

FAMILY: Compositae
BOTANICAL NAME: *Achillea* species
DESCRIPTION: Tiny flowers, usually yellow, come in densely packed racemes at the end of stems that are usually 20-28 in (50-70 cm) long.

The most popular variety used as cut flower is *Achilles filipendula* 'Coronation Gold' and A. 'Moonshine'. Other varieties, which are increasing in popularity, include A. *millefolium* (white or pink), A. *ptarmica* (white) and A. *taygetea* (yellow).
TIME TO BUY: When the florets are fully open, or when the majority of the florets on the cluster have opened.
AVAILABILITY: Summer.
VASE LIFE: 1 week to 10 days.
TRADE CARE: Best kept at 36-41°F (2-5°C). Storage is not recommended.
SUITABLE FOR DRYING

YUCCA
Adam's needle

Yucca filamentosa

FAMILY: Agavaceae
BOTANICAL NAME: *Yucca filamentosa*
DESCRIPTION: Cream-white, bell-shaped flowers, 2-3 in (5-8 cm) long, appear on erect thin spikes. The stems, when cut, reach over 28 in (70 cm) in length.
TIME TO BUY: When the majority of the flowers on the spike have opened.
AVAILABILITY: Summer.
VASE LIFE: 6-8 days.
TRADE CARE: Best kept at 41°F (5°C), although temperatures ranging between 36-41°F (2-5°C) will not harm the flowers.

ZANTEDESCHIA
Calla lily, Arum lily

FAMILY: Araceae

BOTANICAL NAME: *Zantedeschia* species

DESCRIPTION: A solitary flower at the end of a stem, 24-36 in (60-100 cm) long, consists of a large, leaf-shaped spadix that can be white, yellow or pink.

The main varieties are: *Z. aethiopica* (calla lily), with 5 in (12 cm) long spathe; *Z. rehmannii* (pink arum with 3 in (8 cm) long spathe); and *Z. elliottiana* (yellow, with 4 in (10 cm) long spathe). The calla lily is often dyed in a variety of bright colours.

TIME TO BUY: When the flowers are completely open, and just before the spathe begins to turn downwards. If cut too early, they do not open.

AVAILABILITY: All year round, mainly early winter.

VASE LIFE: Approximately 10 days.

SPECIAL HOME CARE: Check the level of water frequently as these flowers are 'heavy drinkers'.

TRADE CARE: Best kept at 41-50°F (5-10°C). Lower temperatures can cause frost damage to the petals. Storage is not recommended.

ZINNIA

Zinnia elegans

FAMILY: Compositae

BOTANICAL NAME: *Zinnia elegans*

DESCRIPTION: Coarse, upright stems carry fully double, dahlia-shaped flowers, 2½-2¾ in (6-7 cm) across, which come in white, pink, red, purple and yellow. The stems, when cut, are over 24 in (60 cm) in length, and carry one flower.

TIME TO BUY: When the flowers have opened. If zinnias are cut too early, they will turn limp.

AVAILABILITY: Summer and autumn.

VASE LIFE: 5-7 days.

TRADE CARE: Best kept at 36-41°F (2-5°C). Storage is not recommended.

SUITABLE FOR DRYING

3

A-Z of
Cut Foliage

HOME CARE TIPS FOR CUT FOLIAGE

Since cut foliage generally lasts much longer than flowers, its handling and care is often overlooked. It is, however, worth taking note of a few tips that will make cut foliage stay fresh for longer.

— The stem ends may be dried up, and unable to take in water. Using a sharp knife or, if the stems are woody, secateurs, cut 1 in (2.5 cm) off the end of the stem. Do not crush the stems, as you may damage the strands that take up the water.

— Clean out the container with soap and water before using. This will ensure the absence of bacteria in the water that can settle in the stems, closing up the water vessels.

— Add a drop of bleach to the water to keep it free from bacteria. Flower preservatives have anti-bacterial agents, and can be used instead of the bleach. The nutrients in the flower preservative are, however, wasted on cut foliage.

— Re-cut the stem ends and change the water frequently, each time cleaning out the vase, and you will be surprised how long and fresh your foliage will last.

ANTHURIUM
Painter's palette, Flamingo flower

FAMILY: Araceae
BOTANICAL NAME: *Anthurium andraeanum*
DESCRIPTION: Heart-shaped, glossy, dark green leaves that vary in size.
AVAILABILITY: All year round. Anthurium leaves are not very common, as they are easily damaged on the plant.
VASE LIFE: Over 10 days.
SPECIAL HOME CARE: Mist with water frequently.
TRADE CARE: Keep away from cold temperatures. Best kept at room temperature. Place in water as soon as possible.

ASPARAGUS PLUMOSUS
Plumosa, Asparagus fern, Lacy fern

FAMILY: Liliaceae
BOTANICAL NAME: *Asparagus plumosus*
DESCRIPTION: Triangular fronds with very flat, feathery foliage. Average length is 16 in (40 cm). There are many different types of plumosus: dark

and light (or blond) varieties, trailing or erect. A good-quality plumosus should end in a tip (known as 'Full Palm'). Some trailing varieties are cut into sections and, although not as attractive, are less expensive.
AVAILABILITY: All year round.
VASE LIFE: Over 2 weeks.
SPECIAL HOME CARE: Plumosus dries up easily: mist frequently with water. When it begins to dry up, it drops its needles, and can be messy.
TRADE CARE: Best kept at 36-41°F (2-5°C), with a high relative humidity of approximately 98 per cent. Plumosus will not last more than 5 days dry; once in water, it will last 10-14 days. High humidity is important to avoid premature needle drop.

Asparagus plumosus is usually sold by the bunch, of 20-30 stems.

ASPARAGUS SPRENGERI
Sprenger fern, Sprengeri

FAMILY: Liliaceae
BOTANICAL NAME: *Asparagus densiflorus sprengeri*
DESCRIPTION: Dark green, needle-like leaves, densely packed on stems that are 16-24 in (40-60 cm) in length.
AVAILABILITY: All year round.
VASE LIFE: Over 2 weeks.
SPECIAL HOME CARE: To avoid premature needle drop, keep it moist by frequent misting of leaves with water, and re-cut the stem ends frequently. When working with sprengeri, it is best to use gloves as it has sharp thorns.
TRADE CARE: Best kept at 36-41°F (2-5°C), with a high relative humidity of 98 per cent. Sprengeri is best kept in water, but can be held at these temperatures for up to 1 week without water in a cold room with high relative humidity.

Sprengeri is usually sold by weight, in bunches of ½-1 lb (250-500 g), or in bunches of 20-25 stems.

ASPARAGUS PYRAMIDALIS
Treefern

FAMILY: Liliaceae
BOTANICAL NAME: *Asparagus pyramidalis*
DESCRIPTION: Similar to sprengeri, but the fronds are more triangular-shaped, and the foliage is more plume-like.

AVAILABILITY: All year round.

VASE LIFE: It is the hardiest of the asparagus ferns, lasting well up to 20 days.

SPECIAL HOME CARE: Keep moist by frequently misting with water.

TRADE CARE: Will last up to 4 weeks, in water, if kept at 36-41°F (2-5°C) with a high relative humidity of 98 per cent. Without water, in these conditions, it can be kept for up to 2 weeks in a cold room with high relative humidity.

ASPARAGUS ASPARAGOIDES
Smilax, Greenbrier

FAMILY: Liliaceae

BOTANICAL NAME: *Asparagus asparagoides*

DESCRIPTION: Long, trailing stems with small, oval, light green leaves. The stems can be several ft (m) long. Several stems are often wired together, both to make longer strands and to make it more resistant to breakage. It is very popular for weddings.

AVAILABILITY: Mainly in the spring and early summer.

VASE LIFE: 7-10 days.

SPECIAL HOME CARE: Smilax is a perishable green that needs constant misting.

TRADE CARE: Best kept at 36-41°F (2-5°C). Unpack as soon as possible. Care should be taken in unpacking, especially if the smilax isn't wired, as it can get tangled and break. The best way to keep smilax is to hang it with its stem end in water; but frequent misting with water is important. It can also be kept soaked with water, lying flat on a piece of plastic.

ASPARAGUS DENSIFLORUS
Ming fern

FAMILY: Liliaceae

BOTANICAL NAME: *Asparagus densiflorus myriocladus*

DESCRIPTION: Tufts of fine, feathery foliage appear profusely on stems that are usually 16 in (40 cm) in length.

AVAILABILITY: All year round.

VASE LIFE: 3-4 weeks.

TRADE CARE: Can be held for 1 week in a cold room, at 36-41°F (2-5°C), with high relative humidity.

Ming fern is usually sold in bunches of 10 stems.

BEAR GRASS

FAMILY: Liliaceae

BOTANICAL NAME: *Xerophyllum tenax*

DESCRIPTION: Long, very thin, grass-like individual leaves, each less than ½ in (1 cm) in width and up to over 3 ft (1 m) in length.

AVAILABILITY: All year round.

VASE LIFE: Over 2 weeks.

SPECIAL HOME CARE: To use in foam, wire a few stems together as the leaves are too thin to be inserted individually into the foam.

TRADE CARE: Best kept in water at 36-41°F (2-5°C).

Bear grass is usually sold in bunches of 25 stems.

BOX

FAMILY: Buxaceae

BOTANICAL NAME: *Buxus sempervirens*

DESCRIPTION: Small, oval, dark green, stiff leaves on woody branches.

AVAILABILITY: All year round.

VASE LIFE: 2 weeks.

TRADE CARE: The vase life of box can be doubled if kept at 36-41°F (2-5°C). It is best always kept in water.

Box is usually sold in bundles.

CHAMAEDORA PALM
Chico palm, Shate palm

FAMILY: Palmae

BOTANICAL NAME: *Chamaedora elegans*

DESCRIPTION: The small palm leaves are no more than 10 in (25 cm) long, with thin fronds, ½-1 in (1-2.5 cm) wide. The main varieties are *Chamaedora elegans* (or collina) with wide fronds and *Chamaedora elegans bella*, with narrow fronds.

AVAILABILITY: All year round.

VASE LIFE: Up to 4 weeks.

TRADE CARE: Best kept in water in a cold room, at 36-41°F (2-5°C); the higher temperature is recommended. Can be kept unpacked for up to 10 days if temperature and humidity are controlled.

Chamaedora palm is sold in bunches of 40-45 stems.

CALATHEA

FAMILY: Marantaceae
BOTANICAL NAME: *Calathea* species
DESCRIPTION: Thin, oval leaves, with a firm, papery texture, that vary in length, size and colour. With interesting shades and lines, these leaves are excellent for arrangements.
AVAILABILITY: All year round.
VASE LIFE: 3-4 weeks.
SPECIAL HOME CARE: They should be placed in water immediately, and misted with water. In darkness they will close, so keep any arrangement with calathea leaves in a light spot.
TRADE CARE: Best kept at a minimum temperature of 41°F (5°C), or the leaves may turn brown. They should be in water at all times. They are often shipped with wet cotton attached to the end of the stem, which should be removed and replaced with fresh water.

CAMELLIA

FAMILY: Theaceae
BOTANICAL NAME: *Camellia japonica*
DESCRIPTION: Popular as cut foliage, camellia has shiny, large green leaves, up to 4 in (10 cm) long, on long, branching stems.
AVAILABILITY: Mainly spring.
VASE LIFE: 1 week.
TRADE CARE: Best kept in water at all times, at 36-41°F (2-5°C). Place in water as soon as possible. The woody stems can be cut with secateurs.

CORDYLINE LEAF
Ti leaf, Palm leaf

FAMILY: Liliaceae
BOTANICAL NAME: *Cordyline terminalis, C. dracaena*
DESCRIPTION: Long leaves, from 1-3 ft (30-100 cm) that are emerald green (green ti) or of a darker green with a red or pink border (red ti). They vary in width from 4-6 in (10-15 cm).
VASE LIFE: 7-14 days.
SPECIAL HOME CARE: Place in water immediately. They can be stapled into interesting shapes and used in arrangements.
TRADE CARE: Best kept cooled, at 36-41°F (2-5°C), with a high relative humidity of 98 per cent. They are often shipped with wet cotton wool attached to the end of the stem. The leaves should be separated on arrival, as they may rot.

CROTON
Codiaeum

FAMILY: Euphorbiaceae
BOTANICAL NAME: *Codiaeum variegatum* hybrid
DESCRIPTION: Colourful, variegated leaves that vary in shape and in size, including combinations of pink, red, orange, and almost black, with green, yellow and white.
AVAILABILITY: All year round.
VASE LIFE: 1 week.
TRADE CARE: If held in water, at 36-41°F (2-5°C), croton leaves will last up to 2 weeks fresh, and keep relatively well as long as they are always kept in water. The leaves are shipped with wet cotton wool attached to the end of the stem; this should be removed as soon as possible, and the stem ends placed in fresh water. Unpack and separate the leaves as soon as possible — they are shipped wet and tend to stick together and rot.

CYCAS PALM LEAVES

FAMILY: Cycadaceae
BOTANICAL NAME: *Cycas revoluta*
DESCRIPTION: Very stiff, short, dark green leaves borne alongside a straight stem that is approximately 20 in (50 cm) in length. It is an expensive green.
AVAILABILITY: All year round.
VASE LIFE: Over 3 weeks.
TRADE CARE: Best kept at 41-50°F (5-10°C). They can be held without water for a few days, but placing them in water as soon as possible is recommended, as they dry up easily.

CYPERUS
Umbrella palm, Palm crown

FAMILY: Cyperaceae
BOTANICAL NAME: *Cyperus alternifolius*
DESCRIPTION: Showy foliage, with long stems, over 3 ft (1 m), that end in a radiating 'umbrella' of approximately 15 thin, green leaves.
AVAILABILITY: All year round.
VASE LIFE: 3-4 weeks.
TRADE CARE: Best kept at 36-41°F (2-5°C). Place in water as soon as possible.

EUCALYPTUS
Silver dollar

Eucalyptus

FAMILY: Myrtaceae

BOTANICAL NAME: *Eucalyptus* species. There are more than 600 types of Eucalyptus, of which only a handful are sold commercially.

DESCRIPTION: The leaves are bluish green to silvery-grey. There are rounded, twin leaves, such as *Eucalyptus cinerea* (silver dollar) and *E. gunnii*; oval leaves, such as *E. stuartina* and *E. populus*; thin, longer leaves include *E. parvifoglia* and *E. nicolli*. Many of these are dyed in a variety of colours.

AVAILABILITY: All year round, though scarce in the summer months.

VASE LIFE: 10 days.

SPECIAL HOME CARE: Misting of the leaves is not necessary.

TRADE CARE: Best kept at 36-41°F (2-5°C), with a high relative humidity of approximately 95 per cent. Whenever possible, ship in water.

Eucalyptus is usually sold in bunches weighing ½-1 lb (250-500 g).

EUONYMUS

FAMILY: Celastraceae

BOTANICAL NAME: *Euonymus japonicus, Euonymus fortunei*

DESCRIPTION: Oval leaves, 2½-2¾ in (6-7 cm) long and 1¼-1½ in (3-4 cm) wide, appear close to and alongside a stem that is usually 20-24 in (50-60 cm) in length. The green form is of a medium green; the variegated form is bright yellow with green.

AVAILABILITY: All year round.

VASE LIFE: Over 2 weeks.

TRADE CARE: Best kept, in water, at 36-41°F (2-5°C). It is not advisable to keep this foliage without water for more than 1 week.

GALAX

FAMILY: Diapensiaceae

BOTANICAL NAME: *Galax aphylla*

DESCRIPTION: Single, round leaves, 4 in (10 cm) in diameter, on short stems. It is dark green or (in the autumn months) reddish-green.

AVAILABILITY: All year round, but less so in spring and summer. It is not readily available, mainly because it is difficult to ship as the leaves are easily damaged.

VASE LIFE: 10 days.

TRADE CARE: Best kept at 36-41°F (2-5°C). Place in water immediately.

GORSE
Furze, Whin

FAMILY: Leguminosae

BOTANICAL NAME: Mainly *Ulex europaeus*

DESCRIPTION: Long, thin stems, bear short, pine-like leaves.

AVAILABILITY: Mainly winter.

VASE LIFE: 1 week.

TRADE CARE: Best kept at 36-41°F (2-5°C). Place in water as soon as possible. Re-cutting of stem ends underwater is especially recommended for this foliage.

HOLLY
English holly, Ilex

FAMILY: Aquifoliaceae

BOTANICAL NAME: *Ilex aquifolium*

DESCRIPTION: Dark green, stiff, spiky leaves in the green form, and green with yellow or white in the variegated forms. Both bear red berries. The branches are woody, and generally long.
AVAILABILITY: November and December.
VASE LIFE: 2 weeks.
TRADE CARE: Holly branches are difficult to place in water because of their bulk and wide branches. Whenever possible keep in water; if not, make sure the temperature is low, 36-41°F (2-5°C), and mist with water frequently to prevent drying up of the leaves. Best kept in a closed box to keep in the moisture.

HUCKLEBERRY
Florist green

FAMILY: Ericaceae
BOTANICAL NAME: *Vaccinium ovatum*
DESCRIPTION: Small, dark green, elliptic leaves appear profusely on stems that generally reach 30in (75cm) in length. It is also sold as 'tips' — the tender top part of the branch. There is also a variety that is brownish-red, commonly known as 'Red Huck'.
VASE LIFE: 2 weeks.
AVAILABILITY: Mainly winter months.
TRADE CARE: Can be kept outside water for up to 2 weeks as long as it is kept at 36-41°F (2-5°C), with a high relative humidity of 95-98 per cent. It is often stored by covering with wet paper.

IVY
Hedera helix

FAMILY: Araliaceae
BOTANICAL NAME: *Hedera helix*
DESCRIPTION: Green or variegated leaves are spaced on long, flexible stems. Ivy is very useful for wedding work and anything that requires trailing. It is sometimes sold cut, in bunches, but it is usually cut from the living plant.
AVAILABILITY: All year round.
VASE LIFE: No more than 5 days.
SPECIAL HOME CARE: Frequent misting with water is recommended.
TRADE CARE: Best kept by misting and placing in a plastic bag, at temperatures between 36-41°F (2-5°C).

LEATHERLEAF FERN
Baker fern, Brake fern, Elephant fern

FAMILY: Aspidiaceae
BOTANICAL NAME: *Dryopteris erythrosora*; and *Rhmohra adiantiformus*
DESCRIPTION: Triangular-shaped fronds, 10-24in (25-60cm) long. There are two main types of leatherleaf that vary slightly in appearance:
Dryopteris erythrosota (Baker fern or American leatherleaf) has stiff, dark glossy leaves.
Rhmohra adiantiformus (African fern, often known as brake fern or elephant fern) has larger, wider fronds, of a lighter green and less stiff than the American types. The name brake fern can cause some confusion, as this is also used to refer to *Nephrolepis exaltata*.
AVAILABILITY: All year round.
VASE LIFE: Over 2 weeks.
SPECIAL HOME CARE: Frequent changing of water, re-cutting of stems, and misting with water are recommended.
TRADE CARE: Best kept at 36-41°F (2-5°C), with a high relative humidity of at least 95 per cent. Under these conditions, leatherleaf will last more than 6 weeks fresh from the moment it is picked — which is why it is often transported by sea containers from America to Europe, a trip that lasts over 10 days. If the fern is to be kept unpacked, it is worth turning the boxes around every 2-3 days, in order to move the water in the box and avoid it settling at one end. Preservative solutions have proved effective at prolonging the life of leatherleaf.
When buying leatherleaf, make sure that the tip of the top fond is stiff enough to be rolled in your fingers; if not, it has been cut too early and will brown prematurely.
Leatherleaf is sold in bunches of 10-25 stems.

LYCOPODIUM
Clubmoss

FAMILY: Lycopodiaceae
BOTANICAL NAME: *Lycopodium taxifolium*
DESCRIPTION: The fork-like branches are covered with bright green, pine-like needles. The stem length is approximately 20in (50cm) when cut.
AVAILABILITY: All year round.
VASE LIFE: Over 1 week.
TRADE CARE: Best kept at 41-50°F (5-10°C), in water.

MAGNOLIA

FAMILY: Magnoliaceae
BOTANICAL NAME: *Magnolia grandiflora*
DESCRIPTION: Oval, dark green leaves, of a leathery texture, are approximately 6 in (15 cm) long, and come on long branches. The stems are woody.
AVAILABILITY: Winter and early spring.
VASE LIFE: 5-7 days.
TRADE CARE: Best kept at low temperatures, 36-41°F (2-5°C), in water. An inexpensive green, used frequently for funeral work in floristry, magnolia is best used as soon as possible as it does not keep well.

MYRTLE

FAMILY: Myrtaceae
BOTANICAL NAME: *Myrtus communis*
DESCRIPTION: There are two types: up to 4 ft (120 cm) tall with large, glossy, green leaves; and smaller leaves on 12 in (30 cm) long stems.
AVAILABILITY: Winter and early spring.
VASE LIFE: 10 days.
TRADE CARE: Best kept at 36-41°F (2-5°C), in water. Under these conditions, myrtle can be held for up to 5 days.

Myrtle is usually sold by weight.

NEPHROLEPIS
Sword fern, Flat fern, Brake fern

Nephrolepis exaltata

FAMILY: Oleandraceae
BOTANICAL NAME: *Nephrolepis* species
DESCRIPTION: There are basically two types that are used as cut foliage:

Boston fern or sword fern (*Nephrolepis exaltata bostoniensis*) that has short, light green leaves alongside a short stem no more than 12 in (30 cm) long. (The name sword fern is also used to refer to polystichum.)

Oregon fern, flat fern or brake fern (*Nephrolepis exaltata cordifolia*) is similar to boston fern but is darker green, and longer. (The name brake fern is also used to refer to African leatherleaf.)
AVAILABILITY: All year round.
VASE LIFE: 5-10 days.
SPECIAL HOME CARE: Mist with water frequently.
TRADE CARE: Best kept cool, at 36-41°F (2-5°C), in water, when it will keep for up to 2 weeks. It should not be kept without water for any period of time. It is often shipped with wet cotton wool attached to the end of the stem.

OREGONIA

FAMILY: Buxaceae
BOTANICAL NAME: *Buxus* species
DESCRIPTION: Similar (and related) to box, it has green leaves variegated with white, similar to a variegated form of *Ficus benjamina*. Oregonia has woody stems.
AVAILABILITY: All year round, although scarce in summer months.
VA LIFE: 2 weeks.
TRADE CARE: Best kept at 36-41°F (2-5°C), in water, for up to 1 week.
  Oregonia is usually sold in branches or bundles.

PALMFAN

Palmetto palm, Fan palm, Cabbage palm

FAMILY: Palmae
BOTANICAL NAME: *Sabal palmetto*
DESCRIPTION: Palm-shaped, with long leaves branching off a single stem that is usually short. The length and width of palmfan is 20 in (50 cm) as an average, but it can vary considerably.
AVAILABILITY: All year round.
VASE LIFE: 1 to 2 weeks.
SPECIAL HOME CARE: Spray constantly with water.
TRADE CARE: Palmfan is best kept at 41-59°F (5-15°C), or at room temperature, in water. Keep away from heat and draughts as it dries up easily. In water, with a high relative humidity, it can be stored for up to 10 days. It is difficult to keep in water, as the stems are short, but it can be kept wet in boxes.

PAPYRUS

FAMILY: Cyperaceae
BOTANICAL NAME: *Cyperus papyrus*
DESCRIPTION: An interesting foliage that has a tuft of shortish, stiff, grass-like leaves that appear at the top of a tall, thick stem.
AVAILABILITY: All year round.
VASE LIFE: 2 weeks.
TRADE CARE: Best kept in water at all times, at between 36-41°F (2-5°C).

PINE-LIKE FOLIAGE

Included under this heading, are the following pine or pine-like greens used in floristry:

Cedar

FAMILY: Pinaceae
BOTANICAL NAME: *Cedrus* species
DESCRIPTION: Flat, lacy foliage, medium green.

White Pine

FAMILY: Pinaceae
BOTANICAL NAME: *Pinus strobus*
DESCRIPTION: Bluish green, stiff needles in multi-branching stems.

Blue Pine or Noble Fir

FAMILY: Pinaceae
BOTANICAL NAME: *Abies procera*
DESCRIPTION: Bluish, stiff needles, rounded on the tips, densely covering branched stems.

Juniper

BOTANICAL NAME: *Juniperus communis*
DESCRIPTION: Medium to light green needles with bright blue berries.

Balsam Fir

BOTANICAL NAME: *Abies balsamea*
DESCRIPTION: Dark green, rounded needles on branching stems, not as densely packed as blue pine.
AVAILABILITY: Winter months; except for cedar, all year round.
VASE LIFE: 2 weeks; except for noble fir that lasts up to 3 weeks.
SPECIAL HOME CARE: Keep in a cool position and, if possible, spray with water frequently to avoid needle drop.
TRADE CARE: Keep at cool temperatures. In winter, when temperatures are below 41°F (5°C), this type of foliage is best kept outside, in a sheltered position, or in a cold room below 41°F (5°C). Avoid any type of heat as this causes drying up and consequent needle drop.

PITTOSPORUM
Pitt, Australian laurel

FAMILY: Pittosporaceae
BOTANICAL NAME: *Pittosporum tobira*
DESCRIPTION: Medium green to light green leaves, in green or variegated forms, come in clusters, on thick, woody stems.
AVAILABILITY: All year round.
VASE LIFE: 1-2 weeks.
TRADE CARE: Best kept at 36-41°F (2-5°C), in water. The leaves dry up and turn brown if it is kept out of water.

Pittosporum is usually sold in branches or bundles.

PODOCARPUS
Yew

FAMILY: Podocarpaceae
BOTANICAL NAME: *Podocarpus macrophyllus*
DESCRIPTION: Podocarpus is conifer-like, with long, slender, flat needles on tall branches.
AVAILABILITY: Winter months.
VASE LIFE: 10 days.
TRADE CARE: Best kept at a minimum of 41-50°F (5-10°C), in water. In these conditions, podocarpus will keep for 1-2 weeks.

POLYSTICHUM
Swordfern, Western fern

The name sword fern is also used to refer to *Nephrolepis*.
FAMILY: Aspidiaceae
BOTANICAL NAME: *Polystichum munitum*
DESCRIPTION: Polystichum is similar to nephrolepis, but has darker, longer, wider leaves, on stems that average 20-24 in (50-60 cm) in length.
AVAILABILITY: All year round, but scarce in summer months.
VASE LIFE: 10-14 days.
SPECIAL HOME CARE: Place in water and mist frequently.
TRADE CARE: Polystichum is the only sword fern-type of foliage that will keep for up to 3 weeks without water at 36-41°F (2-5°C), with high relative humidity. Place in water as soon as possible.

Polystichum is usually sold in bunches of 50 stems.

RUSCUS
Butcher's broom

Ruscus aculeatus

FAMILY: Liliaceae
BOTANICAL NAME: *Ruscus aculeatus; R. hypoglossum*
DESCRIPTION: Dark green, semi-glossy, oval leaves appear along a straight stem. The stem length varies between 16-35 in (40-90 cm).

Italian ruscus (*Ruscus aculeatus*), known also as butcher's broom or smilax ruscus, has smaller, pointed leaves on longer stems.

Holland ruscus (*R. hypoglossum*), known also as Israeli ruscus, has larger, rounder, stiffer leaves than the Mediterranean type.
AVAILABILITY: All year round, but scarce in the summer months.
VASE LIFE: 2 weeks.
TRADE CARE: Best kept at 36-41°F (2-5°C), with a high relative humidity of approximately 95 per cent. It will keep well for up to 10 days without water and, in water, an additional 2-3 weeks.

Ruscus is sold by the stem, either in bunches of 10 stems, or by weight (in bunches of ½ lb, 250 g).

SALAL
Lemon leaf, Papoose

FAMILY: Ericaceae
BOTANICAL NAME: *Gaultheria shallon*
DESCRIPTION: Large, light green leaves on long branches. It is sold as 'tips' — the top, tender part of the branch (known as little john or papoose), or the full length of the branch.
AVAILABILITY: Mainly winter months.
VASE LIFE: 3 weeks.
TRADE CARE: Best kept dry at 36-41°F (2-5°C), when it will keep for up to 10 days.

SCOTCH BROOM
Common broom

FAMILY: Leguminosae
BOTANICAL NAME: *Cytisus scoparius*
DESCRIPTION: Long, needle-like leaves that are rather stiff (they can be gently shaped into curves) with the appearance of stiff grass, reaching a height of over 2 ft (60 cm).

AVAILABILITY: Winter months.
VASE LIFE: 3 weeks.
TRADE CARE: Can be kept for up to 2 weeks in water, at 36-41°F (2-5°C).

A good guide to freshness is to break off a stem; the core should be white. Scotch broom is sold in bundles, by weight.

STRELITZIA

FAMILY: Musaceae
BOTANICAL NAME: *Strelitzia reginae*
DESCRIPTION: Long, oval-shaped, light green leaves, popular in tall arrangements. The leaves are up to 20 in (50 cm) long, on a long sturdy, straight stem. It is uncommon to find a completely healthy leaf — most of them are slightly browned on the tip.
AVAILABILITY: All year round.
VASE LIFE: Up to 2 weeks.
TRADE CARE: Best kept at 36-41°F (2-5°C), in water.

Strelitzia leaves are usually sold with the strelitzia flowers.

4

A-Z of Berries and Ornamental Fruit

HOME CARE TIPS FOR BERRIES AND ORNAMENTAL FRUIT

Most berries are available in the autumn and winter months. When buying berries, look out for any signs of browning on the top berries of the cluster.

— The stems of berried shrubs are woody — it is a good idea to soften the stem tissue by immersing the stem in boiling water for a few seconds. This will not only make the stem easier to cut, but will ease the flow of water up the stem.
— Re-cut, rather than crush, the stem ends, using secateurs, as the stem ends may arrive dried up, and not be able to take in water.
— Use clean containers, and add a drop of bleach to the water, to keep it free from bacteria. Flower food has anti-bacterial agents, and can be used instead of bleach. The nutrients in the preservatives are, however, lost on the berries,
— Frequent re-cutting of the stem ends, and frequent changing of the water in the container, will help keep the berries fresh for longer.

Berries are wonderfully trouble-free and last from 2-4 weeks.

CALLICARPA
Beauty berry, Purple berry

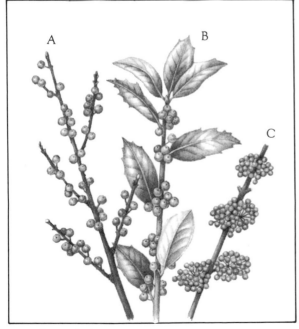

A: *Callicarpa bodinieri*; B: *Ilex aquifolium* 'J.C. van Tol';
C: *Ilex verticillata*

FAMILY: Verbenaceae
BOTANICAL NAME: *Callicarpa bodinieri*
DESCRIPTION: The small, purplish-red berries appear in small, tight clusters up the length of the stem. Callicarpa branches have a section above the top cluster that has no berries. This is not an inferior grade branch, but is a new wood with the flower buds that will produce the berries the following year. A popular variety is *Callicarpa bodinieri giraldi* 'Profusion'.
AVAILABILITY: Winter months.
VASE LIFE: 2 weeks.
TRADE CARE: Keep cool, at 32-36°F (0-2°C).

CAPSICUM
Ornamental pepper, Chilli pepper

FAMILY: Solanaceae
BOTANICAL NAME: *Capsicum annuum*. (The main variety used is C. *annuum* var. C. *frutescens*)
DESCRIPTION: Small, glossy fruit, 1½in (4 cm) wide, that are bright yellow, orange or red, and vary in shape from that of the edible chilli pepper to completely round. They are also grown as pot plants.
AVAILABILITY: Winter months.
VASE LIFE: 7-10 days.
TRADE CARE: Keep at 36-41°F (2-5°C).

ILEX
Holly, English holly

FAMILY: Aquifoliaeceae
BOTANICAL NAME: *Ilex aquifolium*
DESCRIPTION: Bright red or yellow berries appear close to and alongside the stem.

The main varieties derive from *Ilex aquifolium* or are hybrids and have yellow or red berries amidst the leaves. The red berries of *Ilex verticillata* are larger, and appear on leafless stems. In this latter variety, the tip of the branches is cut off as it does not bear berries.
AVAILABLE: November and December.
VASE LIFE: 7-10 days.
TRADE CARE: Keep cool, at 32-36°F (0-2°C).

PERNETTYA

FAMILY: Ericaceae
BOTANICAL NAME: Pernettya mucronata
DESCRIPTION: Tight clusters of small, round berries appear amidst green leaves. The berries can be red, white, purple or pink.
AVAILABILITY: Winter.
VASE LIFE: Up to 2 weeks.
TRADE CARE: Keep cool, at 32-36°F (0-2°C).

PHYSALIS
Cape gooseberry, Chinese lantern

FAMILY: Solanaceae
BOTANICAL NAME: Physalis alkekengi var. frachetii
DESCRIPTION: An orange lantern-like, 2-2½in (5-6cm) long calyx surrounds the orange berry.
AVAILABILITY: Autumn to early winter.
VASE LIFE: 10 days.
TRADE CARE: Best kept at 36-41°F (2-5°C). Re-cut stems on arrival and take care not to crush the berries.
  Physalis is more popular dried than fresh.

SKIMMIA JAPONICA

FAMILY: Rutaceae
BOTANICAL NAME: Skimmia japonica
DESCRIPTION: Tight clusters of bright red berries appear amidst dark green foliage. When the berries die off, small white flowers replace them, and these are popular as fillers in spring arrangements.
AVAILABILITY: Early winter.
VASE LIFE: 10-14 days.
TRADE CARE: Best kept at a minimum temperature of 36°F (2°C), or it will freeze and turn black.

SYMPHORICARPUS
Snowberry

FAMILY: Caprifoliaceae
BOTANICAL NAME: Symphoricarpus albus 'White Hedger'
DESCRIPTION: The glistening white berries are round, up to ½in (1.5cm) in diameter, and appear in small clusters amidst the leaves.
AVAILABILITY: Winter months.
VASE LIFE: 10 days.
TRADE CARE: Keep cool, at 32-36°F (0.2°C).

VISCUM
Mistletoe

FAMILY: Loranthaceae
BOTANICAL NAME: Viscum album
DESCRIPTION: Semi-translucent, white fruits appear in small clusters amidst green leaves. They are sticky to the touch.
AVAILABILITY: December.
VASE LIFE: Mistletoe is not as long-lasting as other berries and ornamental fruit. Its life span is no more than 1 week.
TRADE CARE: Keep cool, at 32-36°F (0-2°C).

Drying Flowers

Dried or preserved flowers are available commercially — but drying your own flowers is not only fun, and will give you a great variety, but is so much cheaper. Some flowers are more easily dried than others; there is a list of the main flowers that can be dried at the end of this chapter. But try out anything: wild flowers or flowers grown in your garden, many of which may dry well.

When choosing flowers to dry, always pick good quality flowers, that are not past their prime: otherwise you might go to all the trouble of drying them, only to have their petals fall off! Choose flowers that are not too 'fleshy', as these contain more water, and will take longer to dry. Remember: the faster the flower dries, the truer the colour will be to the fresh one. Do not dry flowers that are wet; and remove any unwanted leaves or parts of the plant.

Grasses are best sprayed with a fixative (e.g. hair lacquer or other lacquer spray) before drying, or they will disintegrate when dried. Fluffy flowers, or flowers with fluffy seed heads, should also be sprayed before drying.

Some flowers are best wired before drying — either because they have short stems, and longer stems are required, or because their heads are heavy, such as helichrysum, and are likely to flop over and break when dried.

AIR DRYING

This is by far the easiest and most commonly used method. All you need is a well-ventilated room (so that the air can circulate and the flowers will not rot before drying) at an average temperature of 50°F (10°C).

Lying Flat

Some flowers and plants, including most grasses and bamboos, dry best lying flat. Lay the material flat on an absorbant material (such as cardboard, paper or, even, wood) with ample space between the plants so that air can circulate amongst them.

Hanging the Bunches Upside Down From the Ceiling

This is the commonest method. Make up small bunches (of around 5 stems) and hang from the ceiling with ample space between the bunches, to allow for a good air flow. Roses, especially 'necked' bud roses, are best dried this way.

Upright in a Container Without Water

Statice, seed heads and tall grasses are best dried by this method.

Upright in a Container With Water

Other flowers, such as hydrangeas, delphinium and gypsophila, are best dried by placing them upright in a container, with just enough water to cover the stem ends. The stems will absorb the water, which slowly evaporates.

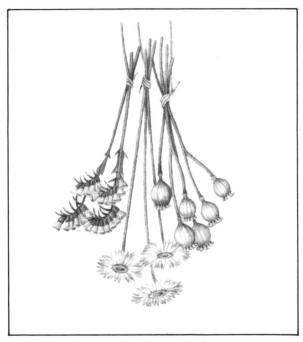

Air drying — hanging bunches upside down

Twined Around a Pole

Climbers, such as clematis, are best dried twined around a pole.

Supported in Chicken Wire

Heavy-headed flowers, such as sweet corn and proteas, are best dried upright, supported on chicken wire, with their stems hanging freely.

DRYING WITH DESICCANTS

Desiccants are substances that draw the moisture out of the plant tissues. The advantage of this method over air drying is that it maintains the colour better, as drying takes less time.

Silica Gel

Drying, using desiccant in a tray

Although the most expensive of the desiccants, silical gel is by far the best, and can be used over and over again. It can be bought from chemists either as white crystals or as crystals with a colour indicator; the latter are recommended as they are blue when dry, and turn pink when they have absorbed moisture. Grind the crystals with a pestle and mortar, and place a layer of crystals, then a layer of flowers, and then cover the flowers with crystals, in a jar or tin that can be sealed. In 2-3 days, the crystals will have turned pink and the flower heads should be firm to the touch. At this point they should be removed, or they will become brittle. To re-use the silica gel, simply place on a tray in a warm oven until the crystals are blue again.

Borax and alum

These have the advantage that they do not weigh as much as silica gel and, therefore, are best suited for delicate flowers, such as anemones, that would be crushed by the weight of a heavier desiccant. These are best mixed with equal parts of sand. Make sure all the desiccant is removed from the flowers, to prevent spotting. Borax or alum drying takes 2-10 days.

Sand

Sand on its own can also be used for drying, as long as it has been strained thoroughly to remove any organic materials or ocean salt. Baking it on an oven tray will make sure that all micro-organisms are killed and that it is completely dry. Sand is heavier and takes long than drying with other desiccants but it is suited for flowers such as dahlias and peonies, whose petals wrinkle when dried with other, lighter desiccants. Sand drying takes several days to up to 4 weeks.

MICROWAVE DRYING

This is the newest and by far the fastest method of drying flowers. Because it works so fast, the colours of the flowers remain very similar to that of the fresh flowers. Choose flowers that are sturdy and have a good water content (i.e. are not limp).

Preheat silica gel in the microwave until the crystals turn blue. Place approximately 2 in (5 cm) of warm silica gel in an oven container, and then the flower. Carefully cover the flower with silica gel, as you would with normal desiccant drying. Set the timer at 1 to 3.5 minutes, depending on the fleshiness of the flowers. If the flower is not drying evenly, interrupt the drying every 30 seconds to rotate the container. If the flower is too brittle, either you have overdone the drying time, or you can place a container with water in the oven. When you remove the container from the oven, leave it for 20 to 30 minutes before removing the flower.

TREATING WITH GLYCERINE

The advantage of glycerine over desiccants is that the material remains supple when dried. The disadvantage is that the colour changes with glycerine — although sometimes you may find that leaves turn into attractive autumn shades. It is mostly recommended for leaves and berries. Glycerine can be bought from chemists.

Instead of removing the water content, glycerine replaces it. Gather sturdy, good material — weak or immature material will collapse with the treatment. Cut the stem ends at an angle, and place them in a container with around 4 in (10 cm) of 1 part glycerine and 2 parts boiling water. Leave them for 3-6 days for soft stems, and up to 6 weeks for woody stems. Check that the level of the solution is covering the stem ends, and brush the tips of leaves with a glycerine/water solution every few days, as it usually does not reach the tips of the leaves.

The plant material is ready when beads of moisture form on the leaf surface, colours change all the way to the tips of the leaves, and the underside of the leaves become oily.

Single leaves can be immersed entirely in a glycerine/water solution, until they change colour. They should then be washed in mild detergent and placed flat on a newspaper to dry.

Glycerine solution can be reused — just add a drop of bleach to keep micro-organisms from forming in it. It does not matter if the glycerine has turned dark.

MAIN CUT FLOWERS THAT CAN BE DRIED

Flower name	Best method	Flower name	Best method
Aconitum	Air drying	Grevillea	Air drying
Alchemilla	Air drying	Gypsophila	Air drying (in water)
Allium	Air drying	Heather	Air drying
Amaranthus	Air drying	Helichrysum	Air drying
Ammobium	Air drying	Helipterum	Air drying
Ananas	Air drying	Helleborus	Desiccant (any)
Anaphalis	Air drying	Heuchera	Air drying
Anemone	Microwave, desiccant (silica gel, borax)	Hydrangea	Air drying (in water), glycerine
Antirrhinum	Desiccant (silica gel)	Iris	Microwave
Astilbe	Air drying	Kangaroo paw	Air drying
Banksia	Air drying (in water)	Lavender	Air drying (preserves the fragrance)
Berries	Glycerine		
(except soft berries, such as mistletoe)		Leontopodium	Air drying
		Leptospermum	Air drying
Carnation	Microwave	Leucadendron	Air drying
(Spray types)		Liatris	Air drying
Carthamus	Air drying	Lily-of-the-valley	Desiccant (any)
Catananche	Air drying	Mimosa	Air drying
Centaurea	Air drying, desiccant	Molucella	Air drying (in water), glycerine (immerse fully)
Chrysanthemum	Microwave		
(small heads are best)		Muscari	Desiccant (silica gel)
Cosmea	Desiccant (borax, silica gel)	Narcissus	Desiccant (silica gel)
Cynara	Air drying	Nigella	Air drying
Dahlia	Dry in sand	Orchids	Microwave
Delphinium	Air drying, desiccant	(small-flowered)	
(mainly larkspur)	(borax)	Ornithogalum	Desiccant (borax)
Dryandra	Air drying	Paeonia	Air drying, desiccant (sand), microwave
Echinops	Air drying		
Eryngium	Air drying, desiccant	Paranomus	Air drying
Foliage	Air drying (in water), glycerine	Protea	Air drying (in water)
		Ranunculus	Air drying, microwave
Freesia	Desiccant (silica gel)	Reseda	Air drying
Gomphrena	Air drying		

Flower name	Best method
Rose	Air drying, desiccant (sand), microwave
Serruria	Air drying
Solidago	Air drying
Statice	Air drying
Sweet william	Microwave
Tagetes	Desiccant (sand, silica gel), microwave
Trachelium	Air drying
Tulip	Microwave
Verbena	Air drying
Xeranthemum	Air drying
Yarrow	Air drying (in water)
Zinnia	Desiccant (silica gel, borax)

FREEZE DRYING

Freeze drying removes moisture from flowers through a process of vacuum freezing. The flowers are laid out onto trays and loaded into large industrial freeze-drying machines. The process takes a few days, depending on the size of the machine and the kind of flowers to be dried.

The advantage of this method is that the freeze-dried flowers do not shrivel or darken. Texture, size and colour remain almost intact. The disadvantage, however, is that freeze-dried flowers do not last very well; they collect moisture from the air and lose colour and crispness quite quickly. They are also very susceptible to moth infestation.

6

Flower Arranging

An elaborate construction of flowers in an urn, and a single flower in a vase, are both flower arrangements. But no arrangement — however simple or complicated — is haphazard, no matter how unstudied it may appear at first sight: knowledge of flower-arranging materials and basic floristry techniques, and confidence in using the basic concepts of design, are all essential for making a flower arrangement that works.

This chapter is intended as a brief guide into experimenting with flowers, to create arrangements that are harmonious within themselves and with their surroundings.

BASIC CONCEPTS OF DESIGN

There are no strict rules in flower arranging, but there are basic concepts of design, which need to be understood to help 'train the eye'. Once your confidence grows with experience, these will come naturally.

What are these 'basic concepts'?

— form;
— movement and rhythm;
— balance and proportion;
— colour and texture.

Form

When you set out to make an arrangement, you will have a definite idea of what its overall shape will be: linear, or roughly triangular, square, fan-shaped or circular.

Steps 1-3 of a flower arrangement. Step 1: placing the structural lines; step 2: placing the focal points; step 3: filling in

It is best to start your arrangement by choosing a long, graceful flower or foliage that will act as the main structural line: its placing will define the overall structure of the arrangement. Visual balance is achieved by placing its tip directly above the centre of the composition (although that is not necessarily above the centre of the container). From there, work with long-shaped flowers, to create lines that define the general shape of the arrangement.

Next, fill in between the lines, place flowers to create the centre or centres of attention. Round and larger flowers or groups of flowers can be used here, placing them close to, but above the rim of the vase. These flowers are the focal points of the arrangement.

Once you are happy with the general effect of the lines and focal points, you can start filling in. Good fillers are small, clustered flowers, berries and foliage, that will fill in and soften shapes, and break harsh lines.

Oriental arrangements are totally linear and, in these, the spaces between the lines, as well as the lines, are viewed as part of the form itself.

Movement and Rhythm

An arrangement of flowers should have movement: it should move the eye around the arrangement, usually from the central axis to other lines, and from there the eye should rest on the focal points. The focal points, therefore, should be bolder than the rest. Most traditional designs have larger and heavier flowers (as well as more intense colours) as focal points, and progressively smaller and finer flowers spread up and from the focal points.

The pace at which the eye moves around the arrangement defines its rhythm: curving and twisting lines, or irregular spacing, can produce a pleasing rhythm, whilst straight lines and repeated, exact spacing can create a monotonous rhythm. The use of, open, half-open and bud flowers, large and small leaves, as well as contrasts in shapes, will all move the eye around the arrangement, creating a graceful, rhythmic movement.

Balance and Proportion

An arrangement should not only be physically balanced, i.e. stable, but should look balanced. Visual balance is achieved by placing heavier-looking flowers at the base of an arrangement, with lighter-looking flowers at the top. Such balance is more easily achieved in symmetrical arrangements, where one side is the mirror of the other half, and the components of each side are the same distance from the central points. Visual balance in asymmetrical arrangements is achieved by a balancing of equal values — like a seesaw: one visually heavy flower can be balanced by a larger quantity of lighter-looking flowers on the other side — or, many flowers near the focal point can be balanced by one heavy flower further away from the focal point, on the other side.

Remember, too, that choice of colour affects visual balance: darker colours look heavier than bright, light colours.

Closely related to the balance of an arrangement is its proportion — however beautiful an arrangement of flowers may be, if it is not in proportion with its container, it will lose its gracefulness. As a rough guide, the height of traditional arrangements is 1.5 to 2 times the height of the container (or the width, if that is greater). In Japanese Ikebana arrangements, the length of the principal line is 1.5 times the width, plus the depth of the container — with the second line being ¾ the length of the first line, and the third line, ¾ the length of the second line.

Colour and texture

The way the eye responds to colour and texture will help to guide you in your choice, and create harmony in your design.

As you know, the primary colours are red, blue and yellow: and mixing these results in pure colours or hues — the purples, the greens and the oranges. If you have a palette of these colours, and mix in black, you will produce shades; white produces tints, and greys produce tones. And all these colours, tints and tones can either be harmonised or contrasted.

When harmonizing colours, you can choose tints, tones and shades of one colour — say pink; or you can choose colours that are adjacent to one another on the colour wheel, say orange/red or orange/yellow.

When contrasting colours, you can combine two colours that are opposite to one another on the wheel, such as yellow and violet. The contrast is striking, and can be softened by using values (shades, tints and tones) of both these colours, and letting one of the contrasting colours predominate.

Colours also play tricks on the eye: dark colours are heavier-looking than light and bright colours — an important point to remember when looking for visual balance. Warm colours (red and orange) make the flowers seem closer than they really are, whilst cool colours (green and blue) make them seem

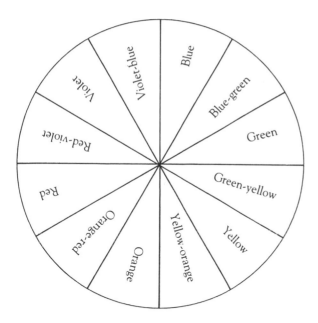

The colour wheel — useful for harmonising and contrasting colours

further away; a useful trick if you want to give visual depth to your arrangement is to place cool colours at the back and warm colours at the front.

Colours are the most powerful element in an arrangement: they have the power to excite, soothe or surprise. They can create a warm, homely atmosphere, or a cool and formal one. The addition of white can soften an arrangement; the addition of green will keep it natural.

Texture is not as powerful as colour, but an interesting contrast in textures can add to the rhythm of an arrangement: from glossy and shiny, to satiny and pearly, to matte and feathery ... Texture is closely related to colour, in that it can determine how much light it reflects. A glossy leaf will appear lighter than a matte one of the same green, that may absorb rather than reflect the light.

CHOICE OF CONTAINER

The design concepts that are applied to the arrangement itself, should be applied to the relationship between the container and the flowers, and to the relationship between the setting and the arrangement. The choice of container takes into account size, colour, texture and shape of the flowers and foliage used, and the setting in which the arrangement is to be placed — neither should overpower the other.

FLOWER-ARRANGING MATERIALS

The resources for flower arranging are as wide as your imagination.

A good knowledge of flowers — their texture, fragrance, colour, how open they should be, how long they last and how they open will allow you to choose compatible flowers for your arrangement. But don't limit yourself only to the florist flowers and foliage mentioned in this book. You can add anything that looks right — be it berries, seed pods, fruit, wild grasses — even bare or budded branches from your garden.

Similarly, don't limit yourself to vases for your containers. Flowers last longer in plastic, glass or ceramic containers, since these are easily cleaned and don't inhibit the action of flower food. But this does not rule out wooden and metal containers — or even terracotta pots and baskets — you can line anything with plastic sheet (if using floral foam), or you can hide a glass or plastic bowl inside almost any basket or pot. Containers are the 'other half' of a flower arrangement, and the container you choose should be in harmony with the arrangement and complement the flowers — so that the eye concentrates on the flowers, not on the container.

FLORISTRY TECHNIQUES

The informality of modern-day living dictates informal designs. Most modern homes and offices are small, practical and far away from nature — so flower arrangements today respond to the need for the natural look. For some occasions, such as the traditional celebrations and festivities, it can be fun to create a more formal, traditional type of flower arrangement.

In most informal, everyday arrangements, you can usually get away without hidden mechanics; but sometimes, no matter how natural you want your arrangement to look — or in fact, to keep your arrangements looking natural — you will have to resort to floristry techniques, to hold a flower in its correct place. In other words, floristry mechanics are not only used for formal, unnatural-looking arrangements, you will find that knowledge of floristry techniques can help you achieve the natural look too.

Many aids are used to keep flowers in their place. The traditional way is netting (or chicken wire, as it is usually called). Choose a wide mesh, so that when it is crumpled, the stems can still pass through the mesh. Crumple the chicken wire to allow sufficient mesh (3-4 layers) so that the stem is secure and won't topple over, and secure it to the rim of the container, so that it does not move around.

Pinholders are useful, mainly for shallow arrangements and to secure thick stems. They are also heavy, and therefore also serve as good ballast inside light-weight containers.

Florist foam has made the life of a flower arranger much easier — allow the foam to soak thoroughly, cut it to fit the shape of the container, and add pieces to the sides to make it tightly fitting. If you are 'building' a top layer onto the base foam, secure it carefully with the use of waterproof florist tape. But remember: foam dries up quickly, so make sure you 'water' it every few days. And one extra word of advice: do not re-use florist foam, as the old holes will make it weak and it will not hold the stems securely.

When making a large arrangement, it is best to use wire netting on its own, or florist foam, secured down with wire netting, as foam on its own will crumble with the weight of the flowers. Large constructions of flowers are made up by using cones, filled with water and/or foam and secured at different levels to sticks.

There are other ways of securing flowers: pebbles, shells and marbles are a fantastic way of holding down flowers in a clear, glass vase. Gravel and stones can be used to raise the foam, pinholder or wire netting — and are also good ballast for top-heavy arrangements. But make absolutely sure that whatever goes into the container is clean, so that no small particles of dirt can get into the stems and obstruct the water flow up to the flowers.

Wiring flowers is a floristry technique that is sometimes overused, resulting in stiff, heavy arrangements, or not used at all by those who consider it taboo as it is not natural. But the overall balance and movement of an arrangement can require that a flower, or group of flowers, is held in a particular position or shape, and this can be achieved by wiring the flowers.

Wires come in different gauges, lengths and types. They are used to either re-inforce a stem, or act as a false stem. As a general rule, use the finest wire that will do the job, and do not overwire. Good wiring should not only be invisible, and kept to a minimum, but should keep the movement and fragility of the flower intact. Wiring is a technique which the beginner can best learn from a good floristry manual.

7

Care of
Cut Flowers
by the Retailer

When cut flowers arrive they are likely to have gone through a certain amount of stress during transport, and may have been without water for some time. The following care tips will bring out the best in the flowers, and prolong their vase life.

RETAIL CARE FOR ALL CUT FLOWERS

Unpack the Flowers

As soon as the flowers arrive, unpack them and loosen up the bunches.

Cut the Ends of the Stems

The flowers may not have been in water since they left the nursery, and the stem ends may have dried up. It is essential to re-cut the ends before placing them in water, or they may be unable to take up water. Use a sharp knife or guillotine or, in the case of woody stems, use secateurs. If possible, re-cut the stem ends underwater, to prevent air travelling up the stem. Crushing or slitting the stems is not advisable.

Remove Lower Foliage

Remove any foliage that would otherwise be underwater, as it may rot, causing bacterial build-up in the water that can clog up the strands in the stem. Remove any excess foliage as well, as valuable moisture can be lost through the leaves.

Place the Flowers in Clean Buckets with Water

Wash out buckets or containers thoroughly, using boiling water and soap, and then rinse out and dry before use. This will prevent any bacteria forming in the water and contaminating the flowers. Use plastic rather than metal containers. Metal containers are more difficult to clean, and the metal can lessen the action of the flower food.

Use warm water (approximately 45°F, 7°C) as it contains less air than cold water and therefore travels up the stems better. Boiling water should only be used to soften up the woody stems.

Water quality can be checked (see Water Quality, page 126).

Use Flower Food

Mix the appropriate flower food or preservatives in the water (see Flower Food, page 119).

Harden the Flowers Before Use

Stand the flowers, in water, in a refrigerated room or cool spot for a few hours before use. They will cool down and become sturdy by taking in water in a cool, humid environment (see Refrigerated Units, page 121).

Keep the Flowers in A Clean, Well-ventilated Environment

Keep flowers in a refrigerated room or cool spot, away from direct sunlight, heat, draughts or air conditioning units, in order to avoid dehydration. They should also be kept away from fruit, vegetables, any fumes and any decaying flowers, as these may cause ethylene gas damage (see Ethylene Gas, page 124).

Finally, everything that comes in contact with the flowers — floors, work benches, buckets, even knives and secateurs — should be kept immaculately clean in order to avoid the spread of post-harvest diseases.

SPECIAL CARE FOR 'TROPICAL' FLOWERS

'Tropical' flowers benefit from extra care, in addition to the above recommendations. Tropical flowers include anthuriums, heliconias, orchids and strelitzias. The extra care advice is given here, rather than repeated under each individual flower.

Tropical flowers are best kept at 45-60°F (7-15°C). Lower temperatures can cause cold damage, resulting in limp flowers or blackening of the petals; higher temperatures will cause premature death and, in the case of orchids, can cause ethylene gas damage (see Appendix III). If you have only one cold room, which is generally the case, see the advice under Refrigeration (Appendix II) on how to maintain these temperatures.

Many tropical flowers arrive with a water vial or wet cotton wool attached to the end of the stem. This should be removed as soon as possible, the stems re-cut, and placed in fresh water with flower preservative. Most such flowers require a high level of humidity. Frequent misting, re-cutting of stem ends, and keeping the flowers away from draughts, fans or air conditioning units, will prevent loss of water.

If orchids look limp on arrival, they may be placed in water — flower head and all — for up to one hour. Similarly, anthuriums can be placed in lukewarm water, but only for a few minutes.

APPENDIX I

Flower Food
and Other Preservatives

FLOWER FOOD

Flower food, or flower preservatives, are used to extend the life of cut flowers. They can be home-made or bought commercially.

Once a flower is cut, the process of photo-synthesis, through which the plant obtains most of its energy, is interrupted. But a cut flower continues to need energy in order to open up and develop to its full potential, and so it is necessary to supply an alternative source of energy. Cut flower food not only supplies the flower with energy: it provides anti-bacterial agents that will keep the water free from bacteria and other micro-organisms, that can form inside the stems, obstructing the flow of water up to the flower. Cut flower food also contains acidifiers, that aid water intake.

The use of flower food has proved effective in extending the life of cut flowers (in many cases, by as much as double). If you do not use flower food, remember to change the water every two days, re-cut the stem ends of the flowers, and clean out the vases thoroughly, as stem blockage is more likely to occur without flower food.

Commercial Preparations

Cut flower food can be bought commercially. The main ingredients of commercial preparations are sugar, to provide the flower with energy, anti-bacterial agents, to kill bacteria and other micro-organisms; and acidifier, to lower the pH in the water (see Appendix V). Secondary ingredients can include hormones and growth regulators as well as wetting agents (to aid water intake).

The chemicals in the commercial preparations vary from one brand to another. An average flower food will have 1 per cent sucrose or dextrose, biocide (200 ppm 8-HQC, 8-HQS, or physaan, or 20-50 ppm silver nitrate or a solution of 5 per cent household dissolved bleach), acidifiers (from 200-600 ppm or 200 ppm aluminium sulphate).

There are many brands available, of which Chrysal and Flowever are perhaps the best known. Some brands are specific to a type of flower, as in the case of bulb flowers and forcing shrubs, as they contain the right amount of sugar suitable for these flower types. If not available, however, overall flower food will do. A new type of flower food, that allows the mixture of freshly-cut daffodils and other flowers, has recently appeared on the market. If this is not available, simply allow the daffodils to stand in water on their own before placing them — without re-cutting — in fresh water with other flowers (see narcissus, Chapter 2).

When using the commercial flower food, simply add a small sachet (or a large tablespoon) of flower food to the water of an average-sized vase. When changing the water of the vase, remember to add more flower food.

Home-made Flower Food

If commercial preparations are not available, flower food can be prepared at home. It is just as effective, although more work, and more expensive. Mix 50 per cent warm water and 50 per cent fizzy lemon drink (Sprite, 7Up or similar), and add 1½ tea-spoons of chlorine (household) bleach. The drink contains sugar, as a source of energy, and citric acid, that will act as an acidifier; the bleach will keep bacteria from forming in the water.

Checklist

— Flower food will not kill bacteria already present in the water, but it will prevent new bacteria from forming. So it is essential to use clean buckets and clean water.
— Do not use metal containers when using flower

119

food. The metal can inhibit the action of the flower food.

— Flower food is to be used in addition to any other type of preservative solution, and any other post-harvest treatment carried out.

— The effectiveness of flower food is in direct relation to the type of water used (see Appendix V).

— Use warm water — not only does it contain less air, and therefore will travel more easily up the stem, but the flower food will mix better in warm water than in cold water.

OTHER PRESERVATIVE SOLUTIONS

Silver Treatment (STS)

Silver treatment (STS) is used to protect cut flowers from ethylene gas damage (see Appendix III). It acts as an antidote, by interfering with the action and synthesis of ethylene by the flower itself. It also contains anti-bacterial agents, so preventing bacterial build-up in the stems. A preparation of silver thiosulphate is mixed with water, and the flowers are placed in this solution for one to 10 hours. It is most effective on flowers that have just been harvested, but is still effective up to three days after harvest. It is, therefore, mostly used at the growers' level, but can in fact be used at all stages of distribution.

Silver treatment on ethylene-sensitive flowers has proved effective at extending the life of the flowers by as much as 75 per cent. It has shown good results in carnations, antirrhinums and gypsophila, amongst other ethylene-sensitive flowers, and is still being tested on other flower types. Flowers that are not very sensitive to ethylene gas damage, such as roses and chrysanthemums, have not been shown to benefit from this treatment.

Commercial preparations include 120g of prismatic sodium thiosulphate and 20g of silver nitrate. It is strongly recommended that you use the commercial preparation rather than mix your own, since the components have to be mixed in the right order and in the right way to be effective.

Pulsing Solutions

Pulsing solutions are used on flowers that have to travel long distances, to load them with sugar and anti-bacterial agents. A high concentration of these are mixed with water and the flowers are treated for a few hours. These solutions are usually used at the growers' level, before shipment, and are effective on certain cultivars only. The commercial preparations have 10-20 per cent sugar, and 150-200ppm biocide.

Bud Opening Solutions

Bud opening solutions are used to speed up the opening of flowers that are in bud or are immature. A concentration of sugar, biocide and acidifier is mixed with warm water and the flowers are placed in this overnight or until the flowers have opened. It is used at all levels of distribution, in warm temperatures with a high relative humidity. The commercial mixture has 1.5 up to 10 per cent sugar, 200ppm biocide and 75-100ppm acidifier.

It is best not to buy bud flowers unless you are completely confident that they will open up well. Remember that many flowers do not open properly if they have been cut at an immature stage, regardless of whether you use bud opening solution or not.

Hydrating Solutions

Hydrating solutions are used to revive limp flowers that are dehydrated. A concentration of acidifiers and wetting agents are mixed in warm water and the flowers are placed in this solution for a couple of hours only. It is carried out at all levels of distribution, and has proved effective at reviving limp roses. If hydrating solutions are not available, some limp flowers (such as roses and orchids) can be hydrated by placing them in water — flower head and all — for a few hours.

It is always advisable to use the ready-made commercial preparations, rather than mixing them yourself, as they have been measured and mixed scientifically, and have clear instructions that will guide you on their use. It can also prove expensive to prepare them yourself, as a certain amount of measuring equipment is needed, such as accurate scales and pH testing equipment.

APPENDIX II

Refrigeration

Heat damage is the no. 1 factor in loss of flowers — keeping flowers cool reduces the risk of loss. Some flowers can be stored for a certain period of time in controlled conditions, without harming or shortening their vase life. Others cannot be stored. But whether for storage or for immediate use, all flowers benefit from proper temperature control.

The advantages of cooling are threefold:

— Proper temperature control will delay the development of flowers, and therefore lengthen their vase life. This is because, at higher temper-

atures, ripening and development are speeded up, resulting in a shorter vase life.

— Flowers also generate heat. Once they have reached a certain temperature, heat build-up increases. This not only encourages the production of ethylene gas, but makes them more susceptible to ethylene gas damage (see Appendix III).

— Finally, flowers at high temperatures are more susceptible to post-harvest diseases, such as botrytis (see Appendix IV).

REFRIGERATION

There are two, quite different, steps in the refrigeration of cut flowers.

Pre-cooling

This method, which is done at the import or wholesale level, takes the heat out of the flowers quickly. One method is simply to unpack the flowers, loosen them up, and place them in a cold room. However, it is not always possible to unpack all the boxes, in which case pre-cooling units are used to remove the excess heat from the flowers, without unpacking them.

Pre-cooling units are used by those who re-ship flowers in their original boxes. The pre-cooling units are fitted onto a wall of the cold room, and the boxes are stacked up against them, with the lateral holes of the boxes against the fans. A flow of cold, humid air will pass through the boxes, removing the heat quickly and effectively. The amount of time the

boxes are left on the pre-cooling unit depends, of course, on the temperature of the flowers — or the amount of heat that has to be removed — the size of the box, the density of pack and the type of flowers.

Cooling

Cooling consists of placing the flowers in a refrigerated unit or cold room, to maintain a low temperature and high relative humidity. There are many types of cold rooms, but there are three requirements that any cold room should fulfil:

— reliable temperature control, with a minimum of variance;
— high relative humidity;
— good ventilation.

TEMPERATURE

A good cold room should have a reliable temperature control, with a minimum of variance.

The temperature differential (TD) is the differ-

ence between the temperature of the coil that is cooling the refrigerator, and the actual temperature of the air inside the cooler itself. The lower this differential — or in other words, the closer the temperature of the coil is to the air temperature of the cold room — the less moisture will be taken out of the air. To achieve a low TD, a large surface coil is needed. The larger the coil surface, the more expensive the refrigeration unit will be, but it is well worth this extra expense.

The ideal average temperature to keep most flowers is between 36-41°F (2-5°C). If the flowers are to be kept in the cold room unpacked (i.e. in their original boxes), then the temperature should be lower, between 34-36°F (1-2°C). These temperatures are the ones best suited to most cut flowers.

'Tropical' flowers are damaged by temperatures below 45-47°F (7-8°C). The average temperature that suits most such flowers is between 45-50°F (7-10°C).

In most cases two cold rooms are out of the question; the solution is to keep the cold room at 36-41°F (2-5°C), and to store the tropical flowers at room temperature. If room temperature exceeds 55-59°F (13-15°C), then these flowers can be cooled down in the cold room for a short time (just enough to bring down the temperature to 45°F, (7°C), keeping them in their boxes, in order to prevent damage.

Since accurate temperature control is so vital in your cold room, this can be controlled by using two thermometers, located in different places in the cold room. The thermometers are best placed at flower level. Small thermometers, that measure the temperature inside boxes of flowers, are also available and these are very useful for establishing what treatment to give the flowers on arrival: if they are too over-heated, to place them in water, or to determine how long to keep them on a pre-cooling unit.

HUMIDITY

Humidity is simply the presence of water vapour in the air. Relative humidity is the amount of water vapour present in the air, compared to the maximum amount that the air can hold.

Humidity is essential for cut flowers and foliage, especially if the flowers are held in a refrigerated unit, as cold dry air can remove moisture in the same way as hot, dry air. Refrigeration, without high relative humidity, will dehydrate the flowers, short-ening their vase life.

Relative humidity of 80-98 per cent is recommended, especially if the flowers are not standing in water. If the humidity level of your cold room is below this, it is not necessary to replace the whole refrigeration unit: adding a humidifier to a cold room is not expensive. Hygrometers, that measure relative humidity, are not expensive to fit or to use.

VENTILATION

We often hear that flowers should be unwrapped and loosened, so that they can 'breathe'. This is true, only for other reasons:

— Circulation of fresh, cool air amongst the flowers will remove excess heat that the flowers may have built up in the box.
— Good ventilation will prevent water (which has evaporated from the flowers) from settling and producing condensation, which can result in botrytis (see Appendix IV).

The air in the cold room should be humid and cool, and its flow should be gentle, in order to avoid drying up the flowers. It is worth noting that ventilation through fans and air conditioning units — as well as proximity to draughts — can dehydrate the flowers.

As a rule, there should be a complete change of air in the refrigerated room every hour.

APPENDIX III

Ethylene Gas

Ethylene gas is a colourless gas emitted by all higher living plants. It is a hormone that speeds up the ripening process of the plant, and therefore cuts down its longevity.
Ethylene gas causes:

— Premature death: flower and petal drop; premature yellowing; and loss of foliage.
— In large quantities, it can stop the development of the flower completely: the flowers shrivel up and turn brown before they open.

Ethylene gas is produced in quantities by:

Other gases such as exhaust, household fumes, smoke and polluted air.
— Most fruit and vegetables.
— Ripening and decaying products — ethylene is given off as part of the natural ripening process and by bacteria or fungi. Dying or damaged flowers especially produce ethylene which also occurs when the flowers are under any kind of stress (such as physical damage or water stress).

The damage caused by ethylene gas is irreversible. Nothing can be done to remedy it, but it is easily avoided:

— Keep flowers away from any sources of ethylene gas, to the extent of removing any damaged or dying flowers or leaves on otherwise healthy stock.
— Maintain low temperatures: not only does ethylene gas occur in greater quantities at high temperatures, but the flowers are more susceptible to the damage when heated. As temperature increases, it takes less ethylene gas to damage the flower.
— Keep flowers in a well-ventilated area, as a continuous change of air prevents ethylene gas from settling in the environment.

Some flowers are more susceptible to ethylene gas than others: carnations, antirrhinums and orchids, for example, need only a small amount of ethylene gas to do the damage, whilst roses and chrysanthemums are more tolerant. The use of STS (silver treatment) has proved effective in protecting some flowers from ethylene gas damage (see Appendix I).

Various types of equipment are available to measure the amount of ethylene gas. The use of ethylene gas scrubbers and absorbers is effective in closed, well-ventilated environments — but they only deal with the ethylene gas they come in contact with as they do not absorb it. However, the same effect can be reached by keeping the flowers cool, in a clean, well-ventilated area.

APPENDIX IV

Botrytis

Botrytis cinerea, or grey mould, is a fungus that forms on flowers causing irreversible damage. Botrytis spores are always present in the air, and only need the right combination of humidity and temperature to germinate, infect the flowers and spread. Even if botrytis spores do penetrate tissue (usually through a wound), they will remain inactive if the temperature and humidity are not right for their development.

The conditions that encourage botrytis are high humidity and high temperature. Alone, high humidity or high temperature rarely results in botrytis infection.

When the humidity level is over saturation point (100 per cent relative humidity), the air cannot hold more moisture and condensation (or free water) will occur. It is only in the presence of free-standing water that botrytis spores germinate — but only if the temperature is above 41-43°F (5-6°C). The early symptoms of botrytis are yellowing leaves, loss of foliage, small white or brown spots on petals and leaves (in dark-coloured petals, the spots are brown and soft; in light-coloured petals, they are white and circular). Once these spots develop into fuzzy, grey mould, the spores are being released into the air, infecting all the surrounding flowers.

To avoid botrytis infection:

— Refrigerated units should not be above 41°F (5°C).
— Wet flowers should never be placed in the cold room.
— The cold room should be well-ventilated.
— The flowers should be loosely bunched, so that the moisture, released by transpiration from the foliage, will evaporate.
— Any damaged, diseased or decaying flowers or foliage should be removed, as botrytis attacks weakened tissues more easily. A good through-put of flowers is therefore essential.
— All that comes into contact with the flowers should be clean, as the infection can spread from decaying material on the floors of cold rooms, or from buckets.
— If botrytis is a constant problem, it is worthwhile checking the post-harvest conditions at your supplier, as well as the working conditions of your cold room.

APPENDIX V
Water Quality

Water can have vastly different characteristics from one area to another. Water type has a direct effect on the longevity and quality of cut flowers. It is therefore important to check your water quality, to see if it needs treatment or modification.

Water type can affect flowers in the following ways:

— Acidic solutions move more readily up the stems than neutral or alkaline solutions. In addition, the amount of alkalinity in the water will affect the action of the flower food and preservative solutions — the more alkaline, the less the capacity of the water to respond.

pH is the measure of acidity and alkalinity: once mixed with flower food, the water for fresh cut flowers should have a pH of 3.5-4.5.

— Water contains a certain amount of minerals (dissolved solids) that can block the strands through which water travels up the stem. The ideal amount of total dissolved solids (TDS) in water for cut flowers is less than 200 parts per million (ppm).

— Some of the minerals and chemicals present in tap water can actually harm the flower: fluoride, for example, causes yellowing of leaves and petal discoloration in some flower types.

The water should be tested frequently to check its purity and pH level. Several laboratories can test your water, but the best method is simply to place some cut flowers in tap water, and others in distilled water, both with and without flower food, and compare the longevity and opening of your flowers. If you find a great difference, it is worth looking into your water quality seriously.

There are basically three ways of modifying or treating water. Any water purifying company will be able to advise you:

— A de-ionizer — the recommended method, as it produces pure water at a relatively low cost of running and installation.
— Filtering the system, which doesn't purify the water well, and is expensive to install.
— Fitting a distillation system, that produces pure water but at a greater cost.

One last note on water quality: if you find that you have 'hard' water, do not use water softeners, as these contain salts, that are harmful to cut flowers.

APPENDIX VI
The Flower Arranger's Cut Flower Guide

Flower Name	Availability	Colour	Description/special design feature
Aconitum	Summer	Dark blue, violet	Hooded flowers on long spikes; tall stem
Adonis	Summer	Yellow	Daisy-like flowers
Agapanthus	Summer	Blue, violet-blue, white	Large round cluster of small flowers; good stem length; true blue colour
Ageratum	Summer	Blue, white	Cluster of small flowers; short stem
Alchemilla	Summer	Yellowish-green	Cluster of small flowers
Allium giganteum	Summer	Purple	Large, stunning, perfectly spherical flower; tall stem
Allium (others)	Summer	Blue, pink, yellow, white	Small round clusters
Alstroemeria	All year	Various	Orchid-like flowers; good stem length
Amaranthus	Summer	Red, creamy green	Unusual shape and colour
Amaryllis	Summer, winter	Pink, red, white	Striking, large flowers at the end of tall stems
Ammobium	Summer, autumn	Pink, red, white	Tiny flowers
Ananas	All year	Pink	Exotic, unusual shape
Anaphalis	Summer	White	Cluster of small flowers
Anemone	Winter, spring	Purple, blue, red	Papery texture; strong contrasting colours; no good with florist foam
Anthurium	All year	Red, pink, white, orange	Exotic, unusual flower; waxy texture; strong colour; long stem
Antirrhinum	Spring, summer	Various	Long stem; bright flowers on tall spike
Aquilegia	Summer	White, pink, yellow, blue, purple	Bonnet-shaped flowers
Arachnis	All year	Bronze	Flowers on thin, long arching stem; unusual colour for an orchid
Aranda	All year	Pink	Delicate orchids on arching stem
Aranthera	All year	Red, yellow, bronze	Small orchids, unusual colours, along arching stems
Asclepias	Summer	Orange	Clustered, small, wavy flowers; short stem
Asconceda	All year	Pink, red	Small orchid flowers along long, thin stem
Aster	Summer	Great variety	Strong, bright colours
Astilbe	Summer	Pink, white, red	Feathery effect; good length
Astrantia	Summer	Red, pink, white	Clusters of small flowers
Banksia	All year	Red, yellow, orange	Exotic, unusual shape
Bellflower	Spring, summer	Blue, white	Snowy flowers along long stem
Bellis	Spring, summer	Various	Daisy-like flower
Boronia	All year	Pink	Clusters of small, waxy flowers
Bouvardia	Spring-winter	Red, pink, white	Clusters of small flowers; bright colours; good length
Brodiaea	Spring, summer	Dark blue, violet	Small flowers in loose clusters
Calendula	Summer	Yellow, orange	Full flowers; strong colours; short stems
Callistephus	Summer	Various	Large full flowers; strong colours
Camellia	Spring	White	Large waxy flower; used for corsages

Flower Name	Availability	Colour	Description/special design feature
Carnation	All year	Variety	Many uses
Carthamus	Summer	Orange	Unusual shape
Catananche	Summer	Blue, purple	Papery, small flower heads; filler
Cattleya	All year	Pink, lavender, yellow, white	Exotic, luxurious orchid
Celosia	Summer, autumn	Red, yellow, orange	Unusual shapes; good length
Centaurea cyanus	Spring, summer	Mainly blue	Papery, small flower head; true blue
Centaurea macrocephala	Spring, summer	Yellow	Large, unusual shape; good length
Chamelaucium	Winter, spring	White, pink	Dense clusters of small, waxy flowers
Cheiranthus	Summer	Various	Cluster of tiny flowers
Chelone	Summer	Pink	Unusual shape; long stem
Chrysanthemum	All year	Yellow, white, pink	Many shapes and uses
C. frutesens	All year	Yellow, white, pink	Daisy flower
C. maximum	All year	White	Large, daisy flower
C. parthenium	All year	White, yellow	Small flowers; long stems
C. segetum	All year	Yellow	Daisy-like flowers
Cineraria	Summer	Various	Daisy-like flowers; strong colours
Cirsium	All year	Red, purple	Small, thistle-like flowers in clusters
Clarkia	Summer, autumn	Various	Profusion of small flowers on spike
Clematis	Summer	Various	Papery texture; cup-shaped flowers
Clivia	Spring	Orange	Bright orange flowers in terminal groups
Coreopsis	Spring, summer	Yellow	Bright, daisy flowers
Cosmea	Summer	Various	Daisy-like flowers
Crocosmia	Summer	Orange	Flowered spike of bright flowers
Cyclamen	Winter	Pink, white	Unusual shape; short stems
Cymbidium	Winter	Various	Large, showy orchids on spike
Cynara	Summer	Purple	Unusual shape; long stem
Cypripedium	Winter	Green, yellow	Small, delicate orchids on spike
Dahlia	Summer, autumn	Various	Bright, showy colours
Delphinium	Spring, summer	Blue, purple	Large, showy flowers closely packed together; long stem
Dendrobium	All year	Purple, white	Small orchids on spike; short stem
Didiscus	Summer	Lavender	Cluster of papery flowers
Digitalis	Summer	Mainly blue	Large hooded flowers, closely packed on spike, long stem
Dill	Summer	Greenish-yellow, white	Fan-like, tiny flowers
Dimorphotheca	Summer	Mainly orange	Daisy-like flowers
Doronicum	Spring, summer	Yellow	Daisy-like flowers
Dryandra	All year	Orange, yellow	Small, brittle flowers on cluster
Echinops	Summer, autumn	Metallic blue	Single, round thistle flower; long stem
Epidendrum	All year	Various	Spike with small, delicate orchids
Eremerus	Summer	Yellow	Tall, erect spikes with tiny, densely-packed, star-shaped flowers; good stem length
Erigeron	Summer	Lilac, purple	Daisy-like flowers
Eryngium	Summer	Metallic blue	Large, unusual thistle-like flowers
Eucharis	All year	White	Delicate, daffodil-shaped flowers in a group at end of stem
Eucomis	Spring	Green-purple	Spike with star-shaped flowers, crowned with a tuft, unusual shape.
Euphorbia fulgens	Winter	Orange, red, white	Recurved spikes with small, star-like flowers.
Euphorbia marginata	Autumn, winter	White	Small flowers amidst foliage at end of stem
Forsythia	Winter	Yellow	Clusters of bright flowers on tall, leafless stem
Freesia	All year	Various	One-sided spikes of flowers; fragrant
Fritillaria	Summer	Yellow, red	Terminal pendant cluster of flowers, crowned with a tuft

Flower Name	Availability	Colour	Description/special design feature
Gaillardia	Summer	Yellow, red	Daisy-like flowers; bright colours
Galanthus	Winter	White	Delicate, hanging flowers at end of short stem
Galtonia	Summer	White-green	Spikes of bell-shaped flowers
Gardenia	Summer	White	Waxen, large, double flowers; good for corsages
Genista	Winter, spring	Yellow, tinted	Small flowers closely packed along leafless stem
Gerbera	All year	Various	Large, striking, daisy-like flower
Ginger lily	All year	Red	Exotic, unusual flower; tall stem
Gladiolus	All year	Various	Colourful flowers along long stem
Gloriosa	All year	Red, yellow	Exotic, unusual shape
Godetia	Spring, summer	Various	Brightly coloured, single and double flowers
Gomphrena	Summer	Various	Small, round flower heads
Grevillea	All year	Red	Unusual, small cone-shaped flowers
Gypsophila	All year	White, pink	Tiny flowers; airy effect
Haemanthus	Summer	Red, salmon, orange	Colourful, unusual flower
Hamamelis	Winter	Red, yellow	Spidery flowers, thickly clustered along leafless stem
Heather	Winter	White, pink, purple, red	Clusters of tiny, bell-shaped flowers
Hebe	Summer	White, violet	Terminal spikes of small flowers
Helenium	Summer	Various	Strongly coloured, daisy-like flowers with prominent centre
Helianthus	Summer, autumn	Yellow	Large, striking daisy-like flowers with large dark centre
Helichrysum	Summer	Various	Small, bright flowers, in a variety of shapes and colours
Heliconia	All year	Red, orange, yellow	Exotic, unusual flowers, of different shapes, on tall, leafless stems
Helipterum	Summer	Pink, white	Daisy-like, straw-textured flowers
Helleborus	Winter	White, pink, purple	Anemone-like, delicate, single flowers
Hesperis	Summer	Lilac, white	Clusters of small flowers along stem
Heuchera	Summer	Mainly red	Clusters of flowers along a thin stem
Hibiscus	Autumn	Red, yellow, pink, salmon	Large papery flowers; bright colours
Hippeastrum	Winter, spring	Pink, white, yellow, red	Striking, large flowers at the end of tall stems
Hosta	Summer	White, lilac	Small flowers on spike, thin stems
Hyacinth	Winter	Pastel colours	Compact short spikes of bell flowers
Hydrangea	Summer	Blue, pink, white	Large, showy flower head; soft colours
Hypericum	Summer, autumn	Yellow	Cup-shaped, delicate flowers
Iberis	Summer	Purple, pink, white	Dense clusters of small flowers
Iris	All year	White, yellow, purple	Striking shape with yellow throat
Ixia	Spring, summer	Red, orange, pink, purple	Bright flowers along long, thin stems
Ixora	All year	Red, orange, pink	Clusters of waxen, tubular flowers
Kangaroo paw	All year	Red, green, yellow	Interesting, unusual, woolly flowers
Kniphofia	Summer	Red, orange, yellow	Tubular flowers, densely packed on spike
Larkspur	Spring, summer	Blue, lilac, pink, white	Large flowers closely packed on spike; long stem
Lavatera	Summer	Mainly pink	Large, delicate-looking single flowers
Lavandula	Summer	Grey-blue	Small flower spikes; very fragrant
Leonotis	All year	Orange	Striking, unusual small clusters
Leontopodium	Summer	White	Small flowers with woolly bracts
Leucadendron	All year	Red, orange	Cone surrounded by colourful bracts
Leucospermum	Autumn, winter	Red, orange, yellow	Unusual, exotic, colourful flowers
Liatris	All year	Purplish-pink	Tall, erect stem packed with tiny flowers
Lilac	Winter, spring	White, pink, purple	Cluster of many small flowers on long straight leafless stem
Lily	All year	Various	Striking, large flowers
Lily-of-the-valley	Spring	White	Small, bell-shaped flowers; bridal work
Linaria	Summer, autumn	Purple, pink	Bright flowers along tall, erect stems
Lisianthus	All year	White, pink, purple	Cupped, anemone-like, delicate flowers

Flower Name	Availability	Colour	Description/special design feature
Lobelia	Autumn, winter	Red, purple	Small flowers, loosely arranged on stems
Lonas	Summer	Yellow	Tight clusters of bright flowers
Lupinus	Summer	Various	Spikes with densely clustered flowers
Lysimachia	Summer	White	Tiny flowers, densely packed on spikes
Mahonia	Winter	Yellow	Bright, dense clusters of tiny flowers
Malope	Summer	Pink, purple, white	Delicate, funnel-shaped flowers
Malva	Summer	White, pink, purple,	Decorative, hibiscus-like flowers; soft colours
Mimosa	Winter, spring	Yellow	Densely-packed, bright fluffy flowers
Moluccella	Spring	Green	Spike with bell-shaped, densely-packed flowers; striking; unusual; long stem
Monarda	Summer	Red, purple, pink	Spidery flowers at end of stem
Muscari	Winter, spring	Blue	Tiny, bell-shaped flowers on thin, short stem; no good for florist foam
Narcissus	Winter, spring	Yellow, white	Both narcissus and daffodils are good for mixed arrangements.
Nerine	Autumn, winter	Red, pink, white	Group of spidery flowers at end of tall stem; striking colour and shape
Nicotiana	Spring	Various	Tubular flowers; strong colours
Nigella	Summer	Grey-blue	Papery flowers amidst dense foliage
Odontoglossum	All year	White, pink, pale yellow, with brown or red spotting	Flat orchid flowers along thin stem
Oncidium	All year	Yellow	Tiny orchid flowers in profusion along long, wiry thin stem
Ornithogalum	Spring, summer	White, tinted (pastel colours)	Tight clusters of star-shaped flowers; striking when fully open
Paeonia	Spring, summer	White, pink, red	Massive, showy flowers, soft colours
Paranomus	All year	Yellow, pink	Unusual, woolly flowers on spikes
Phalaenopsis	All year	Pastel colours	Large, butterfly-like orchid
Phlox	Summer, autumn	White, purple, pink	Terminal clusters of small, bright flowers
Physostegia	Summer	Pink, white, mauve	Tiny flowers, densely set on short spikes
Poppy	Summer, autumn	Various	Papery flower on twisting, wiry stem
Protea	All year	Pink, cream	Unusual, heavy flowers with colourful bracts, often with beards
Prunus	Winter, spring	Pink, white	Delicate-looking flowers along long, woody, leafless stems
Pyrethrum roseum	All year	Various	Daisy-like flowers
Ranunculus	Winter, spring	Various	Delicate-looking, bright colours
Reseda	Autumn	Green, red	Loose clusters of small flowers; unusual
Rose	All year	Various	Variety of sizes and colours
Rudbeckia	Summer, autumn	Yellow	Daisy-like, bright petals, dark centre
Salpiglossis	Summer	Various	Funnel-shaped, interesting flowers
Salvia	Summer	Various	Short, thin stems with small flowers
Saponaria	Summer	Pink, white	Profusion of small flowers
Scabiosa	Summer	Mauve, white	Papery, delicate flower on wiry stem
Schizanthus	Summer	Pink, purple, yellow	Small, orchid-like flower; dense clusters
Schizostylis	Autumn	Red	Striking, small flowers on thin stems
Scilla	Summer	Mainly blue	Small, bright flowers; short thin stem
Sedum	Spring, summer	Various	Tight, large clusters of tiny flowers
Serruria	Summer	White, pink	Unusual, delicate protea flower; bridal
Sidalcea	Summer	Pink, red	Bright flowers on thin, long stems
Solidago	Summer	Yellow	Clusters of tiny flowers; tall stems
Spathiphylum	All year	White	Anthurium-like flower; unusual shape
Statice	All year	Purple, white, yellow	Colourful, tight clusters; good length
Stephanotis	Summer	White	White, waxy flowers; bridal work

Flower Name	Availability	Colour	Description/special design feature
Stock	Spring, summer	Various	Densely-packed spike, large fragrant flowers
Sweet Pea	Spring, summer	Pastel colours	Pea-shaped, delicate flowers; wiry stems
Sweet William	Spring, summer	Various	Clusters of bright colours
Strelitzia	All year	Orange	Unusual, exotic flower; long stem
Tagetes	Summer	Yellow, orange	Colourful, large flowers
Thalictrum	Summer	White, purple	Cluster of small flowers; thin, long stem
Trachelium	Summer	Purple	Umbrella-shaped cluster of tiny flowers on tall, thin stems
Tricyrtis	Summer, autumn	Lavender	Bell-shaped flowers at end of tall stem
Tritonia	Summer	Mainly orange	Bright flowers, similar to freesias
Trollius	Summer	Yellow, orange	Buttercup-like, delicate flowers
Tuberose	Summer	White	Long, thick spike with large fragrant flowers
Tulip	Winter, spring	Various	Good for arrangements and bouquets
Valeriana	Summer	Pink	Cluster of small flowers
Vallota	Summer	Red	Bright, waxy flowers, grouped at end of stem
Vanda	All year	Mainly blue	Large orchid flowers along long stems
Verbena	Summer, autumn	Mainly pink	Small, tight clusters of tiny flowers
Veronica	Summer	Purple	Dense, short spike at end of thin stem
Viburnum	Winter, spring	White	Round, showy group of small flowers
Viola	Spring	Purple, white	Pansy-like flower; short stem
Vuylstekeara	All year	Red, white	Bi-coloured, striking, small orchids along long thin stem
Watsonia	Spring	Mainly pink	Star-shaped flowers on long, thin stem
Xeranthemum	Summer	White, pink, purple	Clusters of tiny papery flowers
Yarrow	Summer	Mainly yellow	Clusters of tiny flowers on long, strong stem
Yucca	Summer	White	Hanging, bell-shaped flowers on long, erect spikes
Zantedeschia	All year	White, yellow, pink	Striking, unusual flower; long stems
Zinnia	Summer, autumn	Various	Brightly-coloured, full flowers

APPENDIX VII

Cut Flower Guide for the Flower Trade

Flower	Openness	Temperature		Special requirements
		°F	°C	
Aconitum	Lower florets open	45-50	7-10	Avoid low temperatures
Adonis	Starting to open	36-41	2-5	Place in water immediately
Agapanthus	One-third of florets open	36-41	2-5	Place in water as soon as possible; handle carefully
Ageratum	Starting to open	36-41	2-5	Place in water immediately
Allium	One-third of florets open	36-41	2-5	Can keep dry for 3-4 days
Alstroemeria	First bud open, rest showing good colour	36-41	2-5	Do not stack, as leaves are easily damaged
Amaranthus	Open	36-41	2-5	Place in water
Amaryllis	One flower opening	41-55	5-13	Avoid low temperature; can keep dry for 1 week
Ammobium	Majority of flowers open	36-41	2-5	Place in water
Ananas	Open	45-50	7-10	Can keep dry for 1 week
Anaphalis	Open	36-41	2-5	Place in water
Anemone	Starting to open	36-41	2-5	Place in water immediately
Anthurium	Open	45-50	7-10	Avoid temperature below 45°F (7°C); can keep dry for 10 days
Antirrhinum	Lower 2-3 florets open	36-41	2-5	Place in water immediately; can keep in water at low temperatures; ethylene gas sensitive
Aquilegia	Starting to open	36-41	2-5	Place in water immediately
Arachnis	Half the flowers open	47-59	8-15	Avoid low temperature; must be in water or with water vial; ethylene gas sensitive
Aranda	Half the flowers open	47-59	8-15	Avoid low temperature; must be in water or with water vial; ethylene gas sensitive
Aranthera	Half the flowers open	47-59	8-15	Avoid low temperature; must be in water or with water vial; ethylene gas sensitive
Asclepias	Majority of flowers open	36-41	2-5	Place in water immediately
Asconceda	Half the flowers open	47-59	8-15	Avoid low temperature; must be in water or with water vial
Aster	Majority of flowers open	36-41	2-5	Place in water
Astilbe	Open	36-41	2-5	Place in water
Astrantia	Majority of flowers open	36-41	2-5	Place in water immediately
Banksia	Open	41-50	5-10	Can keep dry for 1 week

Flower	Openness	Temperature		Special requirements
		°F	°C	
Bellflower	First buds showing colour; none open	36-41	2-5	Place in water immediately
Bellis	Starting to open	36-41	2-5	Place in water
Boronia	Majority of flowers open	36-41	2-5	Place in water
Bouvardia	Two-thirds of florets already open	36-41	2-5	Place in water immediately
Brodiaea	A few florets open	36-41	2-5	Can be held dry for 4 days
Calendula	Open	36-41	2-5	Place in water immediately
Callistephus	Starting to open	36-41	2-5	Place in water
Camellia	Starting to open	45	7	Place in water immediately
Carnation	Beginning to open (in spray varieties, buds showing good colour)	36-41	2-5	Can be kept for up to 1 week dry at 32-34°F (0-1°C) or in water at 36-41°F (2-5°C); ethylene gas sensitive
Carthamus	Burst bud, colour showing	36-41	2-5	Place in water
Catananche	Starting to open	36-41	2-5	Place in water
Cattleya	Open	47-59	8-15	Avoid low temperature; must be in water or with water vial
Celosia	Open	36-41	2-5	Place in water
Centaurea	Half the flowers open	36-41	2-5	Place in water
Cheiranthus	A few flowers open	36-41	2-5	Place in water
Chelone	2-3 flowers opening	36-41	2-5	Place in water
Chrysanthemum	Open	36-41	2-5	Can be held dry at 32-34°F (0-1°C) for 1 week; or in water at 36-41°F (2-5°C)
Cinerarea	Starting to open	36-41	2-5	Place in water
Cirsium	Open	36-41	2-5	Place in water
Clarkia	A few flowers opening	47-55	8-13	Place in water
Clematis	Starting to open	45-47	7-8	Place in water immediately
Clivia	First flowers open	41-47	5-8	Can be kept dry for 4-6 days
Coreopsis	Open	36-41	2-5	Place in water
Cosmea	Starting to open	36-41	2-5	Place in water
Crocosmia	First buds showing colour	36-41	2-5	Can be held dry for 4-5 days
Cyclamen	Flower starting to open	36-41	2-5	Place in water immediately
Cymbidium	All but top flower open	39-45	4-7	Must be in water, or with water vial attached
Cynara	Buds showing colour	36-41	2-5	Place in water
Cypripedium	All but top flower open	39-45	4-7	Must be in water, or with water vial attached
Dahlia	Starting to open	36-41	2-5	Place in water
Delphinium	Most lower florets open	36-41	2-5	Place in water immediately; ethylene gas sensitive
Dendrobium	Most flowers open	47-55	8-13	Must be in water, or with water vial attached; ethylene gas sensitive
Didiscus	Open	36-41	2-5	Place in water immediately
Digitalis	Lower florets	36-41	2-5	Place in water; ethylene gas sensitive
Dill	Open	36-41	2-5	Place in water immediately
Dimorphotheca	Open	36-41	2-5	Place in water immediately
Doronicum	Open	36-41	2-5	Place in water immediately
Dryandra	Open	36-41	2-5	Can be held dry for 4-5 days
Echinops	One-quarter of blooms open	36-41	2-5	Can be held dry for 3-4 days
Epidendrum	Most flowers open	47-55	8-13	Must be in water or with water vial; ethylene gas sensitive

Flower	Openness	Temperature		Special requirements
		°F	°C	
Eremerus	Lower half of florets open	36-41	2-5	Can be held dry for 2-3 days
Erigeron	Starting to open	36-41	2-5	Place in water immediately
Eryngium	Open	36-41	2-5	Place in water
Eucharis	First flowers starting to open, showing colour	45-50	7-10	Avoid cold, keep humidity high; can be held dry for 2-4 days
Eucomis	One-third of florets open	36-41	2-5	Can be held dry for 5 days
Euphorbia	Majority of flowers open	45-55	7-13	Place in water
Forsythia	In bud, smallest sign of colour showing	32-41	0-5	Dry for 1 week at 32-34°F (0-1°C); in water at 39-41°F (4-5°C)
Freesia	One bud open, rest in bud	36-41	2-5	Place in water
Fritillaria	Starting to open	36-41	2-5	Can be held dry for 3 days
Gaillardia	Open	36-41	2-5	Place in water
Galanthus	In bud, showing good colour	47-55	8-13	Avoid cold
Galtonia	Lower florets open	36-41	2-5	Can be held dry for 3 days
Gardenia	Just starting to open	32-36	0-2	Can be held dry for 1 week with high humidity
Genista	Majority of flowers opening	32-41	0-5	Can be held dry for 5 days; ethylene gas sensitive
Gerbera	Open	36-41	2-5	Place in water; handle with care
Ginger lily	Open	47-55	8-13	Can be held dry for 1 week
Gladiolus	Bud, 1-5 florets showing colour	36-41	2-5	In water, at low temperature, can be held 1 week; do not keep dry
Gloriosa	Open	36-41	2-5	Place in water
Godetia	Open	36-41	2-5	Place in water immediately
Gomphrena	Starting to open	36-41	2-5	Place in water
Grevillea	Open	36-41	2-5	Can be held dry for 5 days
Gypsophila	Two-thirds of the florets open	36-41	2-5	Can be held dry for 2 days; ethylene gas sensitive
Haemanthus	Starting to open	45-50	7-10	Place in water immediately
Hamamelis	Starting to open	36-41	2-5	Place in water
Heather	Open	36-41	2-5	Place in water
Hebe	Most flowers open	36-41	2-5	Place in water immediately
Helenium	Majority of flowers open	36-41	2-5	Place in water
Helianthus	Open	36-41	2-5	Place in water
Helichrysum	Open, not showing central disc	36-41	2-5	Place in water
Heliconia	Open	45-50	7-10	Place in water
Helipterum	Open	36-41	2-5	Place in water
Helleborus	Starting to open	36-41	2-5	Place in water immediately
Hesperis	Starting to open	47-55	8-13	Place in water
Heuchera	Half of the florets open	45-55	7-13	Place in water
Hibiscus	Beginning to open	45-55	7-13	Place in water immediately
Hippeastrum	One flower opening	41-55	5-13	Avoid low temperature; can keep dry for 1 week
Hosta	In bud, majority showing colour, only few open	36-41	2-5	Can be held dry for 2-5 days
Hyacinth	Lower petals coloured and starting to open	36-41	2-5	Can be held dry for 2-3 days
Hydrangea	Majority of florets open	36-41	2-5	Place in water immediately
Hypericum	Starting to open	36-41	2-5	Place in water immediately
Iberis	Starting to open	36-41	2-5	Place in water
Iris	Showing colour, not open	36-41	2-5	Can be held dry at 32°F (0°C) for 2 weeks; or in water at 36-41°F (2-5°C); ethylene gas sensitive

Flower	Openness	Temperature		Special requirements
		°F	°C	
Ixia	Showing colour, not open	36-41	2-5	Can be held dry at 32°F (0-1°C) for 3 days; in water at 36-41°F (2-5°C)
Ixora	2-3 flowers open	36-41	3-5	Place in water immediately
Kangaroo paw	Open	41	5	Can be held dry for 4-6 days
Kniphofia	Lower florets open	36-41	2-5	Can be held dry for 2-3 days
Lavatera	Starting to open	36-41	2-5	Place in water
Lavandula	Majority of flowers open	36-41	2-5	Can be held dry for 2-5 days
Leonotis	Open	36-41	2-5	Place in water
Leontopodium	Starting to open	36-41	2-5	Place in water
Leptospermum	Most flowers opening	36-41	2-5	Can be held dry for 2 days
Leucadendron	Open	36-41	2-5	Can be held dry for 1 week
Leucospermum	Open	36-41	2-5	Can be held dry for 4 days; handle with care
Liatris	First (top) blooms open	36-41	2-5	Can be held dry for 5 days
Lilac	Starting to open	36-39	2-4	Can keep dry for 2-4 days
Lily	In bud, showing colour	36-41	2-5	Can be held dry for 2-3 days; or in water for 4-6 days
Lily-of-the-valley	Open	36-37	2-3	Place in water immediately; at 30-32°F (−1-0°C) with rhizome can keep for 2-3 weeks
Linaria	First buds open	36-41	2-5	Place in water immediately, ethylene gas sensitive
Lisianthus	One flower open, many showing colour	36-41	2-5	Can be held dry for 2-5 days; but best in water
Lobelia	In bud, showing colour, no flowers open	36-41	2-5	Place in water
Lonas	Starting to open	36-41	2-5	Place in water
Lupinus	Majority of flowers open	36-41	2-5	Place in water
Lysimachia	Starting to open	36-41	2-5	Place in water immediately
Mahonia	In bud, showing colour	41-50	5-10	Place in water immediately
Malope	Starting to open	36-41	2-5	Place in water
Malva	Starting to open	36-41	2-5	Place in water
Mimosa	Majority of flowers open	36-41	2-5	Can keep dry for 2-3 days ethylene gas sensitive
Moluccella	Open	36-41	2-5	Place in water
Monarda	Starting to open	36-41	2-5	Place in water
Muscari	A few lower flowers open	36-41	2-5	Can keep dry for 3-4 days
Narcissus Daffodils	Goose neck stage	36-41	2-5	Daffodils can keep dry for 7 days
Narcissus	Flowers starting to open	36-41	2-5	Can keep dry for 2-3 days
Nerine	Fully developed buds	41-47	5-8	Can keep dry for 5 days
Nicotiana	Starting to open	36-41	2-5	Place in water
Nigella	Majority starting to open	36-41	2-5	Place in water
Odontoglossum	Half of flowers open	47-59	8-15	Must be in water or with water vial; ethylene gas sensitive
Oncidium	Majority of florets open	47-59	8-15	Must be in water or with water vial; ethylene gas sensitive
Ornithogalum	One-third of buds showing colour, a couple of lower florets open	36-41	2-5	Can keep dry for 7 days; ethylene gas sensitive
Paeonia	Bud, clearly showing colour	36-41	2-5	In bud, can keep dry at 32°F (0°C) for 10 days
Paranomus	Open	36-41	2-5	Can keep dry for 6 days
Phalaenopsis	Open	47-59	8-15	Must be in water or with water vial; handle with care; ethylene gas sensitive

Flower	Openness	Temperature		Special requirements
		°F	°C	
Phlox	In bud, showing colour, no flowers open	36-41	2-5	Place in water immediately
Physostegia	Lower florets open	36-41	2-5	Place in water immediately
Poppy	Petals just starting to break open	36-41	2-5	Place in water immediately
Protea	Open	34-36	1-2	Can keep dry for 1 week
Prunus	Bud, a little colour showing	30-41	−1-5	At 30-32°F (−1-0°C), dry, can keep dormant; in water keep at 39-41°F (4-5°C)
Ranunculus	Just starting to open	36-41	2-5	Place in water immediately
Reseda	Open	36-41	2-5	Place in water
Rose	Petals not separated from flower head	34-41	1-5	Can be held dry for 4 days; but best in water
Rudbeckia	Starting to open	36-41	2-5	Place in water immediately
Salpiglossis	Starting to open	36-41	2-5	Place in water
Salvia	Starting to open	36-41	2-5	Place in water
Saponaria	Most flowers opening	36-41	2-5	Place in water; ethylene gas sensitive
Scabiosa	Starting to open	36-41	2-5	Place in water immediately
Schizanthus	Starting to open	36-41	2-5	Place in water immediately
Schizostylis	A couple of flowers showing colour clearly	36-41	2-5	Can keep dry for 3-5 days; ethylene gas sensitive
Scilla	Few flowers open, most showing true colour	36-41	2-5	Can keep dry for 3-4 days
Sedum	Most florets opening	47-59	8-15	Place in water
Serruria	Open	36-41	2-5	Can keep dry for 3-4 days
Sidalcea	Starting to open	36-41	2-5	Place in water
Solidago	Florets opening, overall colour of bunch still green	36-41	2-5	Can keep dry for 2-5 days
Spathiphylum	Open	47-59	8-15	Can keep dry for 7-10 days
Statice	Starting to open	36-41	2-5	Can keep dry for 1 week
Stephanotis	Open	36-41	2-5	Can keep dry for 4 days
Stock	Half the florets on raceme open	36-41	2-5	Place in water
Strelitzia	Open	47-50	8-10	Can keep dry for 4 days; handle with care
Sweet pea	Starting to open	36-41	2-5	Can be held dry at 32-36°F (0-2°C) for 4-5 days
Sweet william	Most florets open	36-41	2-5	Can be held dry for 5 days; ethylene gas sensitive
Tagetes	Starting to open	36-41	2-5	Place in water immediately
Thalictrum	Most flowers opening	36-41	2-5	Place in water immediately
Trachelium	Few florets open	36-41	2-5	Place in water
Tricyrtis	Bud, showing colour	36-41	2-5	Can keep dry for 2-3 days
Tritonia	First florets showing true colour but not yet open	32-41	0-5	Can keep dry for 5 days at 32-36°F (0-2°C)
Trollius	Starting to open	36-41	2-5	Place in water immediately
Tuberose	First flowers starting to open	47-59	8-15	Place in water
Tulip	Bud, colour showing	32-41	0-5	Can be held dry for 5 days at 32-36°F (0-2°C), or up to 10 days with bulb attached
Valeriana	Open	36-41	2-5	Place in water
Vallota	A couple of flowers open, majority in bud, showing colour	47-59	8-15	Can keep dry for 3-4 days
Vanda	Open	47-59	8-15	Must be in water or with water vial; ethylene gas sensitive

Flower	Openness	Temperature		Special requirements
		°F	°C	
Verbena	Open	36-41	2-5	Place in water
Veronica	Lower florets open	36-41	2-5	Place in water immediately
Viburnum	Overall colour of cluster should be green	36-41	2-5	Can keep dry for 2-4 days
Viola	Starting to open	30-41	−1-5	Can keep dry at 30-32°F (−1-0°C) for 1 week; in water at 36-41°F (2-5°C)
Vuylstekeara	Most florets open	47-59	8-15	Must be in water or with water vial; ethylene gas sensitive
Watsonia	Lower florets opening	36-41	2-5	Can keep dry for 3-4 days; ethylene gas sensitive
Xeranthemum	Most florets open	36-41	2-5	Place in water
Yarrow	Majority of florets open	36-41	2-5	Place in water
Yucca	Majority of florets open	36-41	2-5	Place in water
Zantedeschia	Open, with spathe erect	41-50	5-10	Avoid temperatures below 41°F °C); place in water
Zinnia	Open	36-41	2-5	Place in water

APPENDIX VIII

Bibliography

Arranging Cut Flowers (Ortho Books, San Francisco, Calif., 1985)

Ball Redbook by Vic Ball (Reston Publishing Company, Reston, Va., 1985)

Bloemen Veiling Westland (Naaldwuk, The Netherlands, 1986)

The Book of Tulips by T. Lodwijk (Cassell, London, 1979)

Care and Handling of Cut Flowers by C.L. Holstead (The Society of American Florists, Alexandria, Va., 1985)

Care and Handling of Flowers and Plants (The Society of American Florists, Alexandria, Va., 1985).

Chain of Life by G.L. Staby, J.L. Robertson and D.C. Kiplinger (Dept. of Horticulture, Ohio State University, Columbus, Ohio/Ohio Florists Association, 1978)

The Complete Book of Dried Flowers by Malcolm Hillier and Colin Hilton (Dorling Kindersley, London, 1986)

The Constance Spry Handbook of Floristry by Harold Piercy (Christopher Helm, London, 1985)

Cut Flowers from Bulbs, Grower Guide No. 22 (Grower Books, London, 1981)

Daffodil Varieties (HMSO, 1982)

Exotica by Alfred Byrd Graf (Roehrs Company Inc., 1976)

Freesias, Grower Guide No. 1 (Grower Books, London)

Fresh Flower Book (Floraprint, Lansing, Mich., 1986)

The Garden Book of Heathers by G. Yates (Frederick Warne, London, 1985)

A Guide to Tropical & Semitropical Flora by L.E. Kuck and R.C. Tongg (Charles E. Tuttle Company, 1973)

Introduction to Floriculture by Roy A. Larson (Dept. of Horticultural Sciences, North Carolina State University/Academic Press, 1980)

The Lingarden Guide to Bulbs by D. Papworth (Salamander Books, London, 1983)

The New Art of Flower Design by Deryck Healey (William Collins and Sons, London, 1986)

New Cut Flower Crops, Grower Guide No. 18 (Grower Books, London)

Orchids by A. Bristow (Royal Horticultural Society, London, 1983)

Orchids in Colour by B. and W. Rittershausen (Blandford Press, Dorset, 1979)

Orquideas Ornamentales de Colombia by P. Ortiz, A. Martinez and G. Misas (Carlos Valencia Editores, Bogora, 1980)

Plantes à Fleurs by B. Legge (Nathan Editeur, Paris, 1984)

Des Plantes pour vos bouquets by W. Compson, M. Lockley and P. Marechal (Editions Floraisse, Paris, 1981)

Proteaceae by M. Vogis (C. Struck, Cape Town, South Africa, 1982)

Proteaceae (Protea Colour Prints Pty Ltd, Cape Town, South Africa)

Quality in Cut Flowers, Grower Guide No. 11 (Grower Books, London)

Reader's Digest Encyclopaedia of Garden Plants and Flowers (Reader's Digest Association, London, 1978)

General Index

Botanical and Common Name Index